FOCUSING
BEYOND THE
HORIZON

STEPHEN BISHOP

Published by Zaccmedia
www.zaccmedia.com
info@zaccmedia.com

Published August 2015

ISBN: 9781909824737

British Library Cataloguing-in-Publication Data
A catalogue record for this book is available from the British Library.

Front cover images © Shutterstock.com

CONTENTS

AUTHOR'S NOTE

As with much of London, the area where I live is overflown by a vast number of airliners whisking holiday-makers and travellers to faraway destinations every day of the week. Even if these passengers bothered to look out through the windows it is unlikely that they would be able to distinguish the many landmarks hundreds of feet below. So the silvery thread of the River Lea winding down to the mighty Thames would go unnoticed along with the viaduct and bridge of the Liverpool Street-to-Chingford railway line that crosses it. This would be particularly disappointing.

A century ago that bridge had already spanned the river for 36 years. Railways, roads and rivers were, at that time, the only viable means of popular travel. But in 1909 that was to change significantly, not only for Great Britain but for the world. Because in the arches of that railway viaduct by the bank of the River Lea a young engineer, Alliot Verdon Roe, was fitting together the first all-British aircraft. Flying it across the Marshes for almost 100 feet on the 13th July, it was not only the first powered flight in such a craft, but the continuation of a technological revolution in which this country's designers were to take a significant lead.

World-beating iconic aircraft such as the *Spitfire* fighter, *Lancaster* bomber, *Comet* jet airliner, *Harrier* jump-jet and supersonic *Concorde* (with a little help from the French!), amongst many others, were spawned from that unlikely event in a backwater of London's East End. However, that could simply not be imagined when the wire-braced, yellow cotton-oiled paper contraption struggled into the air.

But A.V. Roe was a man of vision and determination. He saw beyond the immediate and the obvious. Whilst the only tangible reminder of that far-off exploit by the river is one of the ubiquitous 'Blue Plaques' on the viaduct brickwork, perhaps the real memorial to his dreams and foresight is seen in the sky, flying overhead.

So what dreams do you have and how will they be remembered? Because this book is to help us understand that we can each have God-given vision and understanding...to focus beyond the horizon of known possibilities. My prayer is that through studying the life of Samuel in the Old Testament we shall catch hold of such insight so as to bring change not only to ourselves, but to people whom God places alongside us.

Isaiah was inspired to write that those who *'hope in the LORD'* would *'soar on wings like eagles'* (Isaiah 40:31). So let's start to *'soar'*, not physically like A.V. Roe, but spiritually as we focus like Samuel!

1

INTRODUCTION

It Began with a Dream

In bitterness of soul Hannah wept much
and prayed to the LORD.
(1 Samuel 1:10)

READING: 1 SAMUEL 1:1–28

It stood by the bus depot entrance. The community noticeboard was sited so that anyone in that part of Hackney in east London could see it. But they could also contribute since it was a pinboard which enabled messages to be spelt out by means of pins and rubber bands. And the message that caught my eye walking past that late afternoon on the way home from work was simple: 'What if all your dreams came true?'

And all of us dream. It's what makes us human. But it's not down to intelligence, culture, education or social status. If these alone were the drivers then many of the technological, political and social advances around us would still be for the future. But it was because men and women saw beyond their horizons – their natural and physical limitations – that we now benefit from so much in our daily living.

But the greatest dreams have not been in the areas simply of the material and social, but beyond what is appreciated by our senses. Such is the case with the Bible, the means by which God gives us spiritual insight into His nature and purposes. We now have this Book freely available in our own language for individual as well as group consideration. But this has not always been the case. For almost one thousand years it had remained a hidden source, written in Latin, an increasingly inaccessible and distant language. Then someone had a dream. What caused this to arise in the heart and mind of John Wycliffe is not known. But his intention was clear. This was for the Bible to be in English. A theologian, he invited the finest scholars in Oxford to translate St Jerome's Latin Vulgate version into the language of the people. The result – handwritten since this was before the age of the printing press – was distributed by companion dreamers. They were called the Lollards, who took to the mud tracks of medieval England with their concealed manuscripts.

AN OPEN BIBLE

The establishment could not endure this translation being undertaken and the Bibles were outlawed. However, distribution continued and the dream lived on. The latter was epitomised by a verse composed after Wycliffe's death when his ashes were thrown into the River Swift by the authorities who had burnt his exhumed body: 'The Avon to the Severn runs, the Severn to the sea. And Wycliffe's dust shall spread abroad, wide as the waters be.'

The dream was taken a step further by another Oxford scholar at a time when new technology now made it possible for literature to be mass-produced by means of printing. William Tyndale's vision was spelt out to an antagonistic clergyman: 'If God spare my life ere many years I will cause the boy that driveth the plough to know more of the Scriptures than thou doest.' His translation of significant parts of the Bible, which included the entire New Testament, featured turns of phrase that have continued to find a place in colloquial language. He, along with other Reformers, suffered persecution. Finally hunted down and arrested in Antwerp, he was found guilty of heresy and burnt at the stake in 1536. His last recorded words were a prayer . . . and a dream: 'Lord, open the King of England's eyes.'

That was answered only two years later when an injunction, published in the name of King Henry VIII, charged the clergy of the Church to provide an English Bible in each parish. The result was what is known as the Great Bible, based on previous versions which included Tyndale's work.

MORE DREAMS

The dream to possess a Bible, not just to hear it read in church, drove a girl named Mary Jones to undertake a journey. She walked 30 miles across the hills from her Welsh village to buy a copy from Rev Thomas Charles in Bala, her nearest source. The recounting of this incident to a meeting in London led to the vision of making Bibles more widely available. The Bible Society was thus formed in 1804 and currently works in 180 countries spending more than ten million pounds annually in achieving its dream.

Almost a century later the chance meeting of two American Christian businessmen in a hotel realised a dream to make the Bible freely available to fellow travellers. The organisation that they consequently set up was named 'The Gideons'. It broadened its scope so that years later Bibles are now being made available in many places aside from church buildings, including hospital wards, schools, colleges, military camps and prisons, as well as being handed out on streets as part of evangelistic outreach.

All of these men and women, alongside many described in the Bible itself, were dreamers. They were focusing beyond the horizon of what they were currently seeing. And their dreams were birthed in prayer. So our study of Samuel and how we can experience spiritual insight begins with a dream . . . and a prayer. But like many dreams it was also earthed in grim reality.

HANNAH'S MISERY

Hannah was barren. The Scriptural account is quite clear. This was not an accident or an unfortunate turn of events. *'The LORD had closed her womb'* (1 Samuel 1:5). Yet this stark statement was also a stimulus to hope . . . and a basis to dream. For if God had closed her womb, then He could open it!

a stimulus to hope

In the meantime what Hannah saw and experienced with her senses was in contrast to those dreams. The provocation of Peninnah, the other wife of her husband, added to her misery, as did unavoidably seeing the children of her rival – *'all her sons and daughters'* suggests quite a brood (1:4).

What was Hannah's response to all that was going on around and within her? We are simply told: *'In bitterness of soul Hannah wept much and prayed to the LORD'* (1:10). Whilst there are specific warnings in Scripture to guard against such an attitude, it is clearly recognised as a human response. Hannah handled it in the best possible way. She came to God completely up front with how she felt: *'I have been praying here out of my great anguish and grief'*, she explained to the temple priest (1:16). The psalmist similarly encourages us when in this state of turmoil: *'pour out*

4

your hearts to him, for God is our refuge' (Psalm 62:8). As she did this she humbly brought her dream to Him, asking Him to see her misery, committing it to God with a vow.

But as Hannah was stepping out to focus on her dream becoming a reality – although at this stage there was not the slightest hint of a change – the priest observing her in the Lord's temple was focusing on something completely different. On account of her praying silently – *'her lips were moving but her voice was not heard'* (1:13) – he judged her to be drunk. Not an auspicious beginning.

A CONTRAST OF VIEWS

But the subsequent exchange between Hannah and the priest, Eli, contrasts the difference between spiritual focus and human understanding. This clash will be repeated as we look at the life of Samuel. In this instance, Hannah's explanation, which was introduced by stating herself to be one who was *'deeply troubled'*, rather than needing to be rid of wine, resulted in a swift backtracking by Eli. His initial condemnation had been based on visual data and, possibly, past experience . . . and he had jumped to a conclusion. This approach is, sadly, one which we almost inevitably follow. Pausing to ask God for His assessment does not seem to be our natural response.

But, to his credit, Eli's rebuke was replaced with a blessing: *'Go in peace, and may the God of Israel grant what you have asked of him'* (1:17). Hannah graciously received these words as being from God. They were the further means by which her dream – focusing beyond the horizon – was to become a reality.

nothing is impossible with God

Meanwhile, it may be easy for us to be critical of Eli and his speed in making a judgement which could have resulted in this focus being lost, and a dream being extinguished. But even in our own times when God is moving by His Spirit in evident ways such as healing of body, mind and spirit, there may remain a reticence to consider other aspects of life. Support and prayer for those whose focus and dreams arise from other demands and stresses of life may not sit comfortably or seem achievable. But as with Hannah's situation we need to understand that nothing is impossible with God or outside His interest. So perhaps such tangible burdens as financial lack, unemployment, lone parenting, poor education, unchosen singleness, inadequate living conditions, dysfunctional families and bereavement need more open, ongoing support and prayer.

There are more aspects of focusing beyond the horizon to be considered. Some of these will be explored in the following chapters through the life of Samuel, Hannah's first son. He was subsequently described as the 'seer' or prophet. His name meant 'Heard of God'.

And this brings us back to the starting point of focusing beyond the horizon: being open to God-given dreams and bringing them to the One who listens and 'calls things that are not as though they were' (Romans 4:17).

FOR REFLECTION:

- What do you consider were some of the emotions that Hannah was grappling with, as summed up in that phrase, 'bitterness of soul'?
- How does Hannah's natural reaction to adversity help us to realise that the dark experiences of life can somehow point us to God?
- What were the glimmers of hope that Hannah encountered which pointed to her dream possibly becoming a reality?
- Why do you think Hannah held on to her dream even in her hopeless situation?

Our response: Pause and then write down what you sense is a dream from God for yourself, or the church of which you are part.

2

SHARPENED VISION

Then the LORD called Samuel.
(1 Samuel 3:4)

READING: 1 SAMUEL 3:1–21

London commuters owe a debt of thanks to a worm. *Teredo navalis* to be more precise. Without it the traffic in the capital city, along with most of the world's other conurbations, would be completely gridlocked and enshrouded in engine exhaust fumes. But this little creature provided an answer to an otherwise insoluble problem: how to tunnel underground through waterlogged clay.

An engineer, Marc Brunel, discerned the answer. This destructive 'ship worm' that burrowed through boat timbers achieved this feat by secreting a layer of substance that lined the hole it made as it progressed. It provided protection against the possible collapse of the wood. From this Brunel devised the principle of a tunnelling shield behind which a water-resistant, brick-lined tube was immediately constructed, being patented in 1818. It enabled the River Thames to be the first river under which such a tunnel was dug, being completed in 1841. This was the forerunner of deep-level tunnelling undertaken from the latter years of that century and into the next that subsequently enabled millions of passengers to be whisked, unimpeded, around the capital. But it began with someone having the sharpened vision – discernment – to see an application of something that already existed in nature being utilised in civil engineering.

The background to Samuel's life looked promising. God had answered Hannah's prayer and enabled her to have a son – Samuel, who was to be followed by siblings. She carried out the promise that she had made before God: *'I will give him to the LORD for all the days of his life, and no razor will ever be used on his head'* (1 Samuel 1:11). After having weaned him she took the boy, *'young as he was'*, to the house of the Lord at Shiloh, presenting him to Eli the priest. The chapter closes with the simple words: *'And he worshipped the LORD there'* (1 Samuel 1:28).

The narrative in these opening chapters of 1 Samuel is not precise regarding Samuel's age at which he initially served God in the temple under Eli, nor when God first spoke to him. We are only told, *'Each year his mother made him a little robe and took it to him when she went up with her husband to offer the annual sacrifice'* (1 Samuel 2:19). On each occasion there would be a priestly blessing. God was clearly behind those utterances: *'And the LORD was gracious to Hannah; she conceived and gave birth to three sons and two daughters. Meanwhile, the boy Samuel grew up in the presence of the LORD'* (2:21).

GOD WAS STILL SPEAKING

Whatever practical duties Samuel was required to undertake, he had not yet discerned God's voice or been enabled to focus beyond the horizon. However, this was not an issue arising from failure on God's part to speak. These were spiritually dark times when Israel was continually going through the cycle of turning from Him, being oppressed by their enemies, crying out to God for deliverance, and then seeing Him raise up a Judge (see Judges 2:18–19).

But even in that bleak period He was speaking. Eli was himself confronted by a man of God who brought him God's detailed message in respect of his sons' abhorrent and wicked behaviour, and the judgement that would be brought upon the whole family. Further, the account in 1 Samuel 3 of the Lord calling Samuel is prefaced with the statement: *'In those days the word of the LORD was rare; there were not many visions.'* But, clearly, there were some visions. Somehow, somewhere, even in that dark spiritual scenario, the presence of God and His word could be experienced. But it required sharpened spiritual vision to discern Him.

SEEING IN DARK PLACES

The testimony of a Dutch lady, Corrie ten Boom, of her experiences during the Second World War shows that God can work and speak even in such horrendous circumstances. She had been imprisoned in Ravensbrück, a concentration camp, for sheltering Jews from the invading Nazi regime. Having miraculously smuggled a Bible into the camp despite thorough search procedures, she and her sister, Betsie, were able to hold uninterrupted prayer and Bible study meetings with other inmates. They found out later that the reason for the absence of guards and surprise searches was on account of the infestation of fleas in the hut where they were held! During this time Betsie received 'pictures' from God regarding rehabilitation homes that were to be set up when the war was over to help guards and prisoners alike to recover from their trauma. Although she did not survive, Corrie's sister had discerned God's heart – and what was to subsequently come to fruition.

This aspect of God revealing Himself although not in a widespread way is further underlined as a sequel to Samuel recognising God's call. He is described as letting *'none of* [God's] *words fall to the ground'* (3:19). At this stage he was now identifying God's word that gave discernment – and he held on to it. Others may have heard Him speak, but failed to identify and retain what was being said (as described in the Parable of the Sower). Perhaps this is like ourselves when a thought suddenly comes into our minds instigated by the Holy Spirit 'out of the blue' and swiftly departs – unless we take deliberate action to 'drag' it back.

INITIATIVE WITH GOD

What was it that enabled Samuel to be in a place of initially recognising God's voice and having such sharpened spiritual vision? A number of factors are shown in this account in 1 Samuel 3.

1. *Prerogative belonged to God*. It was entirely for Him to decide what He wanted to reveal and when it was to be done, together with the circumstances in which it came about. He spoke to Samuel when, humanly speaking, the 'closed for the day' sign was on the temple door. Similarly we need to be open to God 24/7 because He speaks when He chooses to do so, not when it's convenient for us!

2. *Persistence*. God patiently brought revelation into Samuel's life even though he was not very good, or sensitive, at picking it up. It was only on the fourth occasion that Samuel responded to

God (and then only doing so after receiving some wise advice). Repetition can be a none-too-subtle pointer that God wants our attention!

3. *Personal.* The way in which God brought insight to Samuel was very direct and personal. He spoke to him by name. The revelation was not to be broadcast to everyone and anyone. As if to emphasize the point, Samuel's name was uttered twice (see 1 Samuel 3:10). There are only four other people in the Bible of whom it was recorded that God did this: Abraham, Jacob, Moses, Saul/Paul.

4. *Perspective.* The revelation being brought to Samuel was actually not brand new. Neither Samuel nor we (!) are completely clueless. God was repeating the warning that he had previously brought to Eli through a *'man of God'* (1 Samuel 2:27−36). This related to his sons' wickedness and had evidently gone unheeded. Now God was bringing a new perspective on this situation which had been common knowledge. It was, no doubt, observable even to young Samuel, living, as he was, in close quarters with Eli and his family. Specifically Samuel was given sharpened spiritual vision that 'time was up' and that judgement would now be carried out.

These aspects clearly indicated that the initiative in this whole area of sharpened spiritual vision − of focusing beyond the physical horizon − rested entirely with God. Elisha, a prophet who brought God's word to the nation may years later, was recorded as being approached by a distressed mother. But he did not know the reason for her agitation. The account described his comment on this situation: *'When she reached the man of God at the mountain, she took hold of his feet. Gehazi came over to push her away, but the man of God said, "Leave her alone! She is in bitter distress, but the LORD*

has hidden it from me and has not told me why"' (2 Kings 4:27). But at
least he knew that he didn't know!

OUR RESPONSIBILITY

The onus is on God to bring revelation, but it is our responsibility
to be alert to what is brought to us. When the apostle Paul was
writing to the Christians in Ephesus he laid out what he was
praying for them: *'For this reason, ever since I heard about . . . your love
for all the saints, I have not stopped giving thanks for you, remembering
you in my prayers. I keep asking that the God of our Lord Jesus Christ,
the glorious Father, may give you the Spirit of wisdom and revelation,
so that you may know him better. I pray also that the eyes of your heart
may be enlightened in order that you may know the hope to which he
has called you, the riches of his glorious inheritance in the saints, and
his incomparably great power for us who believe'* (Ephesians 1:15–19;
see also Colossians 1:9–12). In the Old Testament we read of God
encouraging the prophet to be open to revelation: *'Call to me and
I will answer you and tell you great and
unsearchable things you do not know'*
(Jeremiah 33:3).

our responsibility
is to be alert

Samuel needed to be aware and
alert to God's voice and the revelation that He was going to give
him. Eli was able to instigate the former in directing the response
to God's call; Samuel himself facilitated the latter by his openness
and humility. So the ability to discern and focus beyond the
horizon does not operate on a 'blank canvas'. Rather, it is God's
touch upon our lives to distinguish in the light of His Spirit things
that we may already faintly perceive. Many natural scientists and
marine engineers would have been aware of *Teredo navalis*, but
it took one man to see what was offered beyond that creature's
abilities. In the same way, we all need to be keeping our spiritual

'ears' and 'eyes' open to what God may be showing us beyond the physical and material.

THE SMALL THINGS

Zechariah was another prophet who interacted with God in an amazing way! The accounts of these conversations frequently included God asking him, 'What do you see?' and he, in turn, needing to ask God for understanding of the significance of what he was seeing (see Zechariah 1:9; 1:18; 2:1; 4;1; 4:4; 5:1; 5:6; 6:4). On one occasion he heard God speak of the temple being rebuilt by King Zerubbabel, this being a very 'down-market' version of Solomon's impressive structure. But God needed to emphasize that size was not important: 'Who despises the day of small things? Men will rejoice when they see the plumb-line in the hand of Zerubbabel' (Zechariah 4:10). We may easily miss or discard the 'small' promptings, nudges, warnings or thoughts that can flash across our minds and spirits. They may seem insignificant or even foolish. But whatever value we may attach to them, being from God they may well have a significance far beyond our understanding. Ours is the responsibility to have sharpened vision to pick them up and follow them through in order to focus beyond the horizon.

FOR REFLECTION:

- What were the positive aspects of Samuel's environment that could help him discern God's voice?
- What were the negative aspects?
- What steps can we take to be in a better place, physically, spiritually, emotionally and mentally, to pick up on what God is saying?
- How important is it to recognise and respond to what we believe is God's word to us?

Our response: Write down what you sense has been a verse from the Bible which God seems to have underlined for you ... and the steps that you are taking to respond to it.

3

PANIC
MODE!

He cried out to the Lord on Israel's behalf,
and the Lord answered him.
(1 Samuel 7:9)

READING: 1 SAMUEL 7:2-11

'Don't panic!' This was the often repeated 'catchphrase' of Corporal Jones, a character in the BBC Television comedy series entitled *Dad's Army*. It was based on the activities of the Home Guard units that were set up in Great Britain during the Second World War when the country was threatened with invasion. Manned by old soldiers – Jones portrayed one of these with his fighting experiences stretching back to conflicts in the Sudan with the 'Mad Mahdi' half a century earlier – it was also made up of youths too young for conscription, and civilians too disabled.. The plots in the series revolved around various situations that they faced, real and imagined. It was during such stressful events that this cry would be uttered: 'Don't panic! Don't panic!' But as Corporal Jones spoke these words, he was doing the very opposite . . . panicking to an extreme extent!

Whilst as Christians we are reminded of the need not to be anxious or troubled, panic seems to be our 'default' position when under stress. The account in 1 Samuel 7 centres upon the Israelites reacting to bad news. Hearing that their Philistine enemies were poised to attack them, they were *'afraid'*. This term probably encapsulated their mental pictures, based on past experience, of the defeat, devastation and death that threatened. They are in panic mode . . . but Samuel is not.

THE ABSENT GOD

The narrative of those intervening years following Samuel receiving God's call, and then this subsequent national threat, do not include any mention of him or, indeed, of God. Such silence also meant that God's view of the successive events that took place was neither sought nor considered important. The downward slide arising from this omission is starkly recorded: *'Now the Israelites went out to fight against the Philistines'* (1 Samuel 4:1). These enemies were a non-Jewish people-group who had migrated from Crete and lived in the south-western part of Canaan but whom the Israelites had failed to dislodge. Their anti-God stance proved an ongoing threat. The outcome of this attempt to counter their adversary was defeat for Israel. The leaders of Israel sought to find the reason for this . . . but failed to give God space to answer their question! *'The elders of Israel asked, "Why did the LORD bring defeat upon us today before the Philistines?"'* (1 Samuel 4:3). They clearly felt under pressure from this repulse which had cost the lives of about four thousand soldiers.

Being under pressure and not knowing what course of action to take to resolve situations (itself a source of such

18

pressure) can frequently arise. The scenarios in which we experience these feelings are very different from those in the Old Testament. But our response needs to be the same as that of the writer of the Psalms: 'Wait for the LORD; be strong and take heart and wait for the LORD' (Psalm 27:14). This encouragement came on the back of an overwhelming and life-threatening situation against which our problems probably pale into insignificance! But **he knew how** he knew how to respond: 'One thing **to respond** I ask of the LORD . . .' (Psalm 27:4). The psalmist was determined to hold back and discover what God saw of events and what was then to be done in the light of His viewpoint. The account is told of Barry Urquhart, a Christian and the brother of Colin who has been a key figure in bringing renewal back to the Church in Great Britain. Barry ran a building business and was under severe financial strain. He knew that he needed to make a decision concerning whether to continue or close down, the latter clearly affecting his workforce. Not knowing what to do, he shut himself away from everything and everyone for a day, putting himself in a place specifically to hear God on this issue. He believed that God spoke to him in that time about continuing with his work which, indeed, subsequently revived.

NOT WAITING

But those Israelites failed badly in that respect. They did not wait for God. Nor did they summon Samuel. Instead they made a decision, under pressure, with a quasi-religious element: 'Let us bring the ark of the LORD's covenant from Shiloh, so that it may go with us and save us from the hand of our enemies' (1 Samuel 4:3). So they retrieved the ark. This was a chest-type artefact measuring approximately 4 feet long by 2 feet wide, made under God's instruction when the Israelites had been trekking through the desert on the way to the Promised Land. It was overlaid in gold and contained the stone tablets on which were written the Ten Commandments. It was normally housed in the temple at Shiloh. Now it was to be taken into battle as a talisman.

Any warnings or reservations by Eli the priest concerning this action with regard to the ark were not recorded. Perhaps he failed even to comment on that unwise action. His sons, however, were complicit with this decision and accompanied the ark into the clash against the Philistines. The outcome of this action was succinctly described. *'So the Philistines fought, and the Israelites were defeated and every man fled to his tent. The slaughter was very great; Israel lost thirty thousand foot soldiers. The ark of God was captured, and Eli's two sons, Hophni and Phinehas, died'* (1 Samuel 4:10–11).

A TRAGIC STAGE

However, there was further disaster to come. When the news of the fate of the ark reached Eli, he fell backwards off his chair by the side of the gate in Shiloh and broke his neck. His daughter-in-law, also hearing about the ark, went into premature labour, being fatally overcome by her pains. She somehow managed to give her baby son a name: *'Ichabod, saying* [meaning] *"The glory has departed from Israel"'* (1 Samuel 4:21). A poignant title summing up this tragic stage of Israel's history.

Twenty years then elapse. God miraculously steps in so that the ark is returned to Israel, being held in an outpost. At this point there is a turning back to God by the nation. The Israelites somehow realised that their desperate situation arising from the continuing threat of these Philistines was, at its root, a spiritual one. (How many of our own problems could actually be traced back to the same source?) It could therefore not be resolved by means of their own resources or religious schemes. It needed God. But they took some time in reaching that conclusion!

RETURN TO GOD

At this point Samuel reappears. He brings an unequivocal demand: 'If you are returning to the LORD with all your hearts, then rid yourselves of the foreign gods and the Ashtoreths and commit yourselves to the LORD and serve him only, and he will deliver you out of the hand of the Philistines' (1 Samuel 7:3). There is a positive response from the people to this direction in ceasing the immoral practices that were involved in the 'worship' of these pagan deities. Samuel then draws the nation (or its representatives) together and undertakes a symbolic act in pouring out water before the Lord. Humbling themselves before God in fasting, they openly confess their sin.

But then an unexpected but dreaded event occurred. The Philistine hoards reappear: 'the rulers of the Philistines came up to attack them.' Upon hearing this news the response of the Israelites was to be 'afraid'. This brings us back to our starting point. That description of the Israelites' reaction probably understated all the negative feelings arising from those events that had engulfed them 20 years previously. They were seriously panicking!

DON'T PANIC

Whereas the Israelites are, understandably, absorbed by the overwhelming physical danger, Samuel is focusing beyond the horizon. He refuses to accept that what he is seeing is going to have an inevitable result. Instead he continues turning to God. In response to the people's plea he offers up a

he continues turning to God

sacrifice and cries out to God. And the result? '. . . *and the* LORD *answered'* (1 Samuel 7:9).

The narrative does not elaborate on the length of time that elapsed between Samuel crying out and God's response. All that can be deduced was that it took place *'that day'*. The fact is that God answered, just as he had answered Hannah's prayer many years previously and, before that, Isaac the patriarch's prayer, in respect of Rebekah his childless wife. God answers prayer . . . beyond the horizons of our expectations or abilities; when we are in desperate need, as were the Israelites when oppressed by successive enemies and he raised up Judges to bring deliverance. Even when we are in 'panic mode'. The psalmist seemed to experience the latter many times. But on each occasion he witnessed to God's loving response. *'To the* LORD *I cry aloud, and he answers me from his holy hill'* (Psalm 3:4). *'I sought the* LORD, *and he answered me; he delivered me from all my fears'* (Psalm 34:4). *'When I called, you answered . . .'* (Psalm 138:3).

But there could well be a time lapse in such an answer coming. The psalmist knew about this too. His response was to pause. *'I waited patiently for the* LORD; *he turned to me and heard my cry'* (Psalm 40:1). Fast forward several quantum technological leaps and I too was having to wait. A computer problem (from which no-one seems exempt) meant that I was not able to access some urgent work that had been emailed to me. I was therefore trying to work out who I could approach for help in terms of borrowing their hardware at short notice. Worrying, praying to God, and then worrying again are my default responses to trouble! On this occasion God's answer came before I could resort to worry and panic mode in earnest. It also came unexpectedly . . . as I was cycling to work the following morning. A name suddenly came to my mind: someone I could (and did subsequently and successfully) ask for help, and within the necessary time frame.

FOCUS ON GOD

God's answer to Samuel's cry was to send thunder . . . from beyond the horizon. *'But that day the LORD thundered with loud thunder against the Philistines'* (1 Samuel 7:10). The narrative does not give any detail as to the form or intensity of this event or even if it involved a literal and severe storm. But what is described is the dramatic effect: *'. . . and threw them into such a panic* [that word again!] *that they were routed before the Israelites.'* Pursuit and slaughter of Israel's implacable enemies then ensued.

Samuel had not been oblivious to what was going on around him and the threat that existed. But he refused to accept that what he saw was inevitable. He had the spiritual insight to focus on God in prayer. A lesson we all need to learn: don't panic, but pray.

FOR REFLECTION:

• What made the threat of the Philistine attack such a serious danger to the Israelites, and in what other terms could their response be described?

• What elements of adverse situations might cause us to react negatively?

• What enabled Samuel to stand firm when everyone else was reacting in such a negative way?

• What type of situations have caused you to respond in fear and possible panic?

Our response: Write down a couple of verses from the Bible that have helped you to remember the power and protection of God.

4

MARKERS

*Then Samuel took a stone and set it up
between Mizpah and Shen.*
(1 Samuel 7:12)

READING: 1 SAMUEL 7:12–17

'Blue Plaques' are now commonplace. In London they are particularly used to identify the place of birth or residence of a notable person. But in a Paris park I spotted a French equivalent marking a particular event. Mankind's horizon was lifted – almost literally! It was a seismic change which we cannot appreciate. Two men defied gravity and left the surface of this earth without any mechanical means of support or lift. The latter was provided by invisible, but tangible, hydrogen gas filling their 'grand balloon'. This brave achievement in December 1783 may be little remembered – but it was a necessary stepping stone in aviation history. And that memorial stone ensured that its importance was not forgotten.

TANGIBLE SIGNS

Sadly, many of the events in the Old Testament are relegated to occasional sermons or books. Their importance is ignored. But Samuel knew that a marker was needed to help the Israelites themselves remember their past . . . and how God had stepped in beyond their horizon of possibility or ability. So he literally set up a stone for that purpose. '*Then Samuel took a stone and set it up between Mizpah and Shen. He named it Ebenezer, saying: "Thus far has the* LORD *helped us"'* (1 Samuel 7:12). It's unfortunate that Charles Dickens' well-known novel, *A Christmas Carol*, should take up that name and use it in a particularly negative light ('Ebenezer Scrooge'). The name itself means 'Stone of help'. It was a reminder that God had not only been aware of the Israelites' desperate situation, but powerfully intervened to help them achieve victory over their Philistine enemies.

MODERN MARKERS

Such markers can have very practical implications. This was the case when the leadership team in my local Anglican church sensed that God was directing action to be taken to redevelop the church site. The particular verse which energised this step was from Isaiah: '*Enlarge the place of your tent, stretch your tent curtains wide, do not hold back; lengthen your cords, strengthen your stakes'* (54:2). Over a three-year period there was extensive construction work resulting in a designated youth and children's annex (including resources for those with special needs), an atrium coffee shop, an office suite and conference facilities. At every stage there were answers to prayer which God used to keep us focused on Him. Not least of these was the release of finance – almost entirely through the church congregation and supporters – at a time of economic downturn.

But the completion of this building project was not the end. It was acknowledged that the bricks and mortar were only the beginning. This was because the rebuild was seen as the means by which people in the community – near and far – were to be reached with the Good News of Jesus. But the structures were, and continue to be, a marker and encouragement, an 'Ebenezer'. What God had done to bring this redevelopment into reality is enabling the church to focus beyond the horizon of work that He is yet to do in people's lives, both physically and spiritually.

UNLIKELY SETTING

But 'markers' can also be found in unlikely settings. One such example refers to the power by which God brought about victory over the Philistines by means of thundering *'with a loud thunder'*. It is located in an unlikely setting many miles (and many centuries later) from the original scene. Overlooking the impressive Scarborough Bay in North Yorkshire, England, are the ruins of an old church. Inscribed on one of the remaining arches are these words from Psalm 93: *'Mightier than the thunder of the great waters, mightier than the breakers of the sea – the LORD on high is mighty'* (verse 4). God has His way of prompting people to set up such markers in unexpected places!

SIGNPOSTS FOR OTHERS

However, Samuel did not stop at erecting a stone marker. Having stepped into the limelight and directed God's people back to Him at Mizpah, his role as 'Judge' (or deliverer) became established in a more high-profile setting: *'Samuel continued as judge over Israel all the days of his life'* (1 Samuel 7:15). The practical way in which this was carried out is then described. *'From year to year he went on a circuit from Bethel to Gilgal to Mizpah, judging Israel in all those places'* (verse 16).

In addition there are indications that he was responsible for setting up a provision sometimes termed a 'school of the prophets'. Certainly such institutions were flourishing many years later at the time of those great prophets Elijah and Elisha. The narrative in 2 Kings 2:1–17 describes *'the company of the prophets at Bethel . . . Jericho . . . fifty men of the company of the prophets'* (see also 2 Kings 4:38; 6:1.) Prior to these events, back in the time of Samuel, the existence of *'prophets'* was described when a *'procession'* of them met the king-to-be, Saul. As foretold, he then himself prophesied with them (1 Samuel 10:5–6). The obvious failure of Eli and his sons in their appointed responsibilities as priests could well have been a stimulus to such 'schools' being set up. It would have been Samuel's desire to imbue the hearts and minds of others with his perception of God's righteousness and power, and His will for His people to focus beyond the horizon, seeing situations and people as He saw them. Setting up the facility for this to be achieved was itself a 'marker', not now in stone but a living 'letter', as the apostle Paul was subsequently to describe his Corinthian readers (see 2 Corinthians 3:2–3).

PERSONAL SIGNPOST

This chapter of 1 Samuel closes with reference to a third 'marker'. *'But he* [Samuel] *always went back to Ramah, where his home was, and there he also judged Israel. And he built an altar there to the LORD'* (7:17). This could be seen as a personal reminder of who God was, of His plans and purposes beyond what could presently be perceived. Whilst, as individuals, we may have particular events and tangible reminders of what God has done for us which point to horizons beyond, there are two 'markers' which can apply to all of us.

The first is baptism. Various church traditions operate differently in respect of this practice. However, it seems clear that the New Testament pattern took this as involving full immersion of adult believers. The Greek word is *baptizo* and means to 'dip' or 'immerse' as when cloth is placed in a dye. The description of Jesus coming *'up out of the water'* (Matthew 3:16) and the apostle Paul writing of being *'buried with him* [Christ] *through baptism'* (Romans 6:4) would validate this view – notwithstanding my own involvement in an Anglican church which also practises infant sprinkling: that's a conversation for another time! In spiritual terms it is not only a vivid statement to the world that a person has accepted Jesus Christ as their Saviour and Lord, but a declaration of belief in what is yet to come. Paul adds to the previous explanation as follows: *'Or don't you know . . . just as Christ was raised from the dead through the glory of the Father, we too may live a new life'* (6:3–4). It is a significant 'marker' of the old life being *'buried'* with Christ, and rising up out of the baptismal waters to demonstrate the *'new life'* that is now being lived . . . and horizons yet to be focused upon, culminating in the assuring statement: *'If we have been united with him like this in his death, we will certainly also be united with him in his resurrection'* (6:5).

ANOTHER PERSONAL 'MARKER'

A similar approach can be seen in the second personal 'marker'. This is our participation in Communion, or the Lord's Supper. Whilst Jesus commanded this to be undertaken *'in remembrance of me'* (Luke 22:19), it was to be done *'until he comes'* (1 Corinthians 11:26). Here was a pointer to an event we are also yet to experience, one that is beyond the horizon. But as we celebrate, with humility and thankfulness, the sacrifice that Jesus made on the Cross, it is with our spiritual eyes focused ahead. This is done alongside others; a reminder that we need the support of 'fellow focusers'. *'Because there is one loaf, we, who are many, are one body, for we all partake of the one loaf'* (1 Corinthians 10:17).

Samuel may have seemed to be on a lonely vigil as he scanned the spiritual horizon, but with these 'markers' and knowledge of those who had gone before, he would have been aware that he was but one of *'a great cloud of witnesses'* (Hebrews 12:1) to the invisible God and His work that was yet to be physically apparent.

FOR REFLECTION:

• What personal 'markers' could you devise as a reminder of God's help?

• What might be viewed as a contemporary equivalent of those 'schools of the prophets'?

• What is your experience of baptism and how can it be a help in looking forward?

• How can Communion be celebrated in a way which makes a greater spiritual impact?

Our response: Write down some way in which a verse from the Bible which has encouraged you in the past can be used as a 'marker' to be kept in view for the future.

5

EYES ON
THE BALL

Samuel told all the words of the LORD to the people
who were asking him for a king.
(1 Samuel 8:10)

READING: 1 SAMUEL 8:1–22

The 2014 World Cup soccer tournament in Brazil treated a worldwide audience to a spectacle of footballing skills and techniques, played in hot and humid conditions. Yet all these abilities could be said to rely on one key factor, the way in which the players always kept their 'eyes on the ball'. A fine example of this was the Argentinian striker Lionel Messi, when he struck a wonderful free kick from outside the penalty area and into the back of the Nigerian goal – his approach and concentration on the ball, oblivious to the noise and activity around him, summing up that lesson.

This, of course, is reflected in many other sports. The Test Cricket batsman stroking the ball with effortless ease and timing to the mid-off boundary for four runs. The Wimbledon tennis finalist connecting her racket to the ball and delivering a glorious half-volley down the court line for a winning point. The Ryder Cup golfer accurately judging distance and direction when putting his ball from the edge of the green and into the final hole.

The writer to the Hebrews in the New Testament similarly stressed the need for us to *'fix our eyes on Jesus'* (Hebrews 12:2). Sadly, this is what the Israelites failed to do in the period when Samuel was God's prophet to the nation. Instead their eyes were focused on what they saw around them. The result was that their elders came to him with a request: *'appoint a king to lead us, such as all the other nations have'* (1 Samuel 8:5). It was this action that caused him to turn again to God in prayer.

A PROBLEM

There had been two immediate causes that gave rise to this disappointing request. The first was on account of Samuel himself. What moved him to appoint his two sons as Judges to succeed him, and then to maintain them in that role, is not explained. Their unsuitability is clearly disclosed: *'But his sons did not walk in his ways. They turned aside after dishonest gain and accepted bribes and perverted justice'* (1 Samuel 8:3). It appeared that the same failings that had befallen Eli and his two sons were being repeated. So the elders of Israel were up front: *'You are old, and your sons do not walk in your ways'* (verse 5). Clearly Samuel could do nothing about the former, and did not seem to consider the latter as being something that could be effectively changed. So there was a definite problem.

One of the factors that needs to be taken into account when we face difficulties is the need to be real. There can be the temptation to ignore, downplay or refuse to accept adverse situations or their implications. They can be too painful or demanding. This reaction is neither healthy nor wise. The psalmist frequently detailed the pressures that he was experiencing and saw the necessity of doing so as a step to then presenting them to God, before looking to move on. He once wrote: *'I cry aloud to the LORD; I lift up my voice to the LORD for mercy. I pour out my complaint before him; before him I tell my trouble'* (Psalm 142:1–2). He's not burying his head in the sand in that scenario!

LOOKING AROUND, NOT UP

But having seen the problem in front of them – and commendably facing up to it as well as confronting Samuel – those elders of Israel took their 'eyes off the ball'. This was the second cause of their erroneous request to Samuel. Instead of looking up to God, they looked around them.

What they saw was the other nations around them each being headed up by a king – this was seen as the solution to their problem of leadership. *'Now appoint a king to lead us, such as all the other nations have'* (1 Samuel 8:5). A tangible threat had been an impetus to this request. Samuel subsequently recounted: *'But when you saw that Nahash king of the Ammonites was moving against you, you said to me: "No, we want a king to rule over us"'* (1 Samuel 12:12). We, so easily, adopt the same attitude. We see what other people around us are doing when in pressing **we push God off our 'radar'** circumstances and look to emulate them. So when financial pressures arise, budgets are readjusted and church offerings are reduced. Or when schedules get squeezed, prayer time and Bible reading gets put aside. When feeling under pressure we may try to relax in front of the television or computer instead of turning to God. It's very easily done. Whilst these few examples may be generalisations, they do point to a 'default' position – do what others do. As a result, like those elders of Israel, we push God off our 'radar'.

THE FULL PICTURE

Unfortunately, 'selective' vision was also in operation. Although the elders had come to Samuel with their agenda, they had failed, or refused, to notice certain other factors. Looking at the picture as a whole presented a more sobering assessment. Having a king brought with it a 'price tag'. This was clearly spelt out, in some detail, by Samuel when he came back to them after praying to God: '*This is what the king who will reign over you will do: He will take your sons and make them serve with his chariots and horses, and they will run in front of his chariots. Some he will assign to be commanders of thousands and commanders of fifties, and others to plough his ground and reap his harvest, and still others to make weapons of war and equipment for his chariots. He will take your daughters to be perfumers and cooks and bakers. He will take the best of your fields and vineyards and olive groves and give them to his attendants. He will take a tenth of your grain and of your vintage and give it to his officials and atttendants. Your menservants and maidservants and the best of your cattle and donkeys he will take for his own use. He will take a tenth of your flocks, and you yourselves will become his slaves*' (1 Samuel 8:11–17). No holds are barred in that disclosure . . . and all this, it might be said, was on a good day!

That lengthy description of the outcome of appointing a king to rule the nation, clearly spelling out the consequences, ended with an even more severe warning: '*When that day comes, you will cry out for relief from the king you have chosen, and the* LORD *will not answer you in that day*' (1 Samuel 8:18). The final answer of those elders revealed their spiritual state.

They refused to listen. They looked around and wanted a king like everyone else.

REJECTING GOD

When Samuel had prayed to God following that initial approach, he had been consoled by being told that it was not he, but God, who was being rejected. Despite the miraculous deliverance from slavery in Egypt and victory over many enemies, the Israelites kept turning from God . . . time and time again: *'As they have done from the day I brought them up out of Egypt until this day, forsaking me and serving other gods, so they are doing to you.'* Then, perhaps with a tone of exasperation, God directs Samuel: *'Now listen to them; but warn them solemnly and let them know what the king who will reign over them will do'* (1 Samuel 8:8–9). *'Listen to them and give them a king'* (verse 22).

It takes effort and determination, along with support from others, to keep our eyes on God. The world in which we live can be totally absorbing and distracting. It so easily squeezes us into its mould. But the reality, and the way ahead, is not found in the immediate and the obvious. It is found in a deepening relationship with God and focusing on Him. As we do so, He helps us to focus beyond the horizon and see *'the race marked out for us'* (Hebrews 12:1).

FOR REFLECTION:

- What are particular sources that drag us back to patterns of behaviour adopted by this world, taking our eyes away from God?
- How can they be countered?
- What does Psalm 73 tell us about those whose lives are based on 'doing their own thing' without regard for God?
- How does that psalm bring out a better focus on God's character?

Our response: Write down a verse from Psalm 73 in which you find an encouraging focus on God's character.

6

SEEING
STARS

Now the day before Saul came, the LORD
had revealed this to Samuel.
(1 Samuel 9:15)

READING: 1 SAMUEL 9:1 – 10:1

'Two men look out through the same bars; one sees the mud, and one the stars' (Rev. Frederick Longbridge, taken from his religious tract, 'A Cluster of Quiet Thoughts').

The account in 1 Samuel 9 of Israel's first monarch being appointed contrasts the viewpoints of the two principal characters, Saul and Samuel. Like the quotation above, they were living in the same environment but seeing very different goals. The former was concentrating on locating lost donkeys. Samuel was looking for a national leader.

The initial description of Saul actually puts him in a good light. He's obedient and responsive to his father and diligent in searching for these straying livestock. In addition he's ready to act on the suggestion of his servant who points out that the *'man of God'* lives in the locality and might advise on what direction to take. Although these are positive qualities, they still show that he sees 'mud' and is not appreciative of 'stars' ahead.

PRACTICAL ACTION

This is in contrast to Samuel who is open to God, so that we read: *'Now the day before Saul came, the LORD had revealed this to Samuel: "About this time tomorrow I will send you a man from the land of Benjamin. Appoint him leader over my people Israel . . ."'* (9:16). Although not stated, it seems that Samuel was directed to a specific location, the town (in the *'district of Zuph'*) where there was going to be a sacrifice at the high place – he was going to bless it and then join the people in eating (see 1 Samuel 9:12–13). The girls whom Saul had met specifically stated that this event was taking place *'today'*, with Samuel having *'just come'*. God's revelation to Samuel had required practical steps to be taken in order for him to be in the right place at the right time. It was then that he would be 'focusing beyond the horizon'.

Taking practical action as shown by Samuel is often described in the Bible. This was the prelude to seeing God work in extraordinary ways. But such steps were not without risk or ridicule! God required Noah to build an ark. Abraham had to prepare for a sacrifice. Jeremiah needed to go to the potter's house. Moses was directed to point his staff over the Red Sea. The Israelites were instructed to walk round the walls of Jericho. The servants in Cana were told to pour out the contents of the water jars. The disciples were commanded to throw out their nets. Each of these, alongside many others, was a step (sometimes literally!) of faith. It preceded divine intervention. Some of these actions were in themselves very mundane . . . others were seriously 'going out on a limb'.

Perhaps Samuel's visit to that town fell into the former category. But it still required prompt and **it preceded divine intervention** specific obedience; otherwise the 'chance' meeting with Saul would not have taken place – the heir-apparent would simply have returned home to allay the fears of his father who, he reckoned, would now be worrying. The time and space needed away from distracting family and work surroundings to anoint and counsel Saul would no longer have been available.

CLUELESS

When the two men subsequently met, Samuel knew at once from God, *'This is the man I spoke to you about'* (9:17). Saul, however, didn't have a clue! He asked: *'Would you please tell me where the seer's house is?'* Samuel's reply, *'I am the seer'*, confirmed his identity. One wonders whether it was uttered with an inward sigh! Saul clearly had little or no conception of the spiritual dimension, or concern about the seismic change in leadership that the nation was seeking. He was not aware that Samuel lived in the vicinity and had no idea of his identity even though he was God's appointed Judge – and had been for years. So what planet had Saul been living on during this time?

NOT THE SAME HYMN SHEET

Saul's initial response to Samuel's declaration that he was the *'desire of Israel'* (meaning, he was the king that the people were wanting) was similar to Gideon's when told by the Angel of the Lord that he was to be God's deliverer for the nation (see Judges 6:15). He immediately stated his poor pedigree and how it rendered him unsuitable: *'But am I not a Benjamite, from the smallest tribe of Israel, and is not my clan the least of all the clans of the tribe of Benjamin?'* (1 Samuel 9:21). This was a further indication that he was not 'singing from the same hymn sheet' as Samuel . . . or God. The repeated examples from the history of God's people even up to that point showed that the Lord often worked in the lives of those who seemed least qualified, gifted or able, either in respect of their personal circumstances or background.

move our focus to worship Him

Either Saul was ignorant of this fact or too absorbed in himself – perhaps more of the latter as subsequent events were to reveal.

The would-be king not only failed to see those 'stars' but would have found it difficult to view himself at any point beyond the 'mud'. This is not to say that God is oblivious to our experiences and feelings. But we can only be fulfilled people, *'conformed to the likeness of his Son'* (Romans 8:29), as we move our focus to worship Him, looking for His Kingdom purposes worked out in our lives. Saul needed to aspire to be God's anointed earthly king. We are to aspire to be God's *'chosen people, a royal priesthood, a holy nation, a people belonging to God, that you may declare the praises of him who called you out of darkness into his wonderful light'* (1 Peter 2:9).

GOD'S PURPOSE

There is a hint that leadership was something of which Saul was aware and a role he wanted. Samuel's opening comment to him had included the following: *'. . . and in the morning I will let you go and will tell you all that is in your heart'* (1 Samuel 9:19). Following the feast that had been arranged in the town at which the seat of honour had been given to Saul, the necessary talk from Samuel had taken place. He wasted no time in trying to refocus Saul's mindset from Kish to kingdom, from donkeys to destiny. It took all night to make a start (9:25–26). Subsequent events indicate that it was never fully achieved.

But that is God's heart for us . . . to live so that we see beyond the *'donkeys'* and the 'mud' that preoccupy us and to focus more on what he wants for ourselves and those around us. This is what the apostle Paul was inspired to write: *'I keep asking that . . . God . . . may give you the Spirit of wisdom and revelation, so that you may know him better. I pray also that the eyes of your heart may be enlightened'* (Ephesians 1:17–18).

The amazing thing is that Saul had started that day looking for lost livestock . . . and ended it finding a God-given purpose. As we put effort into focusing beyond the horizon, our circumstances may be moved by God very quickly, with little warning... if any.

FOR REFLECTION:

- Why do you think Saul was so preoccupied with finding those lost donkeys?
- What aspects of our present age could be equated with those donkeys and the preoccupation that can arise?
- Although no details are given in this account, what do you think Samuel was particularly talking to Saul about during that night following the feast and preceding the actual anointing the following day?
- What steps can we take to enable us to refocus from the 'mud' and the 'donkeys' onto the God-given purposes for our lives?

Our response: Look at Hebrews 12:1–2 and write down some of the things that might 'hinder' you in living out a God-focused life.

7

FEET ON
THE GROUND

When Samuel brought all the tribes of Israel near,
the tribe of Benjamin was chosen.
(1 Samuel 10:20)

READING: 1 SAMUEL 10:9–25

It was a mistake. In fact it was a bad one. The evangelistic and Bible-teaching literature printed in the Russian language was meant to omit any logo or hint of its origin. But somehow all the design work and templates had incorporated the normal appendage: 'Gospel Printing Mission' with its UK contact details underneath. Compounding the error, large quantities of the resultant printed leaflets and booklets were posted out before it was realised that they included this compromising information. And this was at a time when the USSR was a belligerent, anti-God, anti-West, one-party state. The Soviet customs officials and security services would be particularly alert to such Christian 'propaganda'.

The Mission had gone out on a limb in producing such literature, believing that this was directed by God. Indeed, described as a 'faith' undertaking, the whole Mission was run on the basis of 'focusing beyond the horizon', with finance and resources being received in answer to prayer rather than obtained on commercial principles and associated marketing techniques.

By the time the mistake was realised there was nothing that could be done. There was only a metaphoric 'shrugging of shoulders'; nothing in the mode of 'taking authority' or viewing it as particular 'spiritual warfare'. Feet were kept firmly on the ground – the future was uncertain and the only view taken was that God would have to be trusted for the outcome.

Fast forward a few years and 'perestroika' and 'glasnost' suddenly hit the headlines. The 'Iron Curtain' was in meltdown . . . and the Gospel Printing Mission was suddenly in receipt of numerous requests for Christian literature posted from far-flung corners of the previously 'evil empire'. How had these pleas for vital and urgent resources been directed to GPM? Because of the 'mistake' described above! This enabled Russian Christians and churches to learn of a source of supply through the address details, the original tracts and booklets having been distributed in clandestine ways miles from their original point of arrival.

PRACTICAL STEPS

'Focusing beyond the horizon' can actually be very down to earth and practical. It is not the reserve of the 'super spiritual', highly proficient, got-it-all-together-type Christian who never has to grapple with doubt, failings and uncertainty. All of us struggle in our walk with God for various reasons much of the time. So a step-by-step, down-to-earth approach is often the best way ahead, however laboured it may seem.

Returning to the account in 1 Samuel, we see that the prophet kept his feet on the ground and took practical steps necessary for

Israel's first king to be identified. This was in spite of the badly mistaken direction that the nation had chosen. He first of all *'summoned'* the people of Israel to a location used for previous significant gatherings, Mizpah. This was located about seven and a half miles north of Jerusalem (which was still occupied by their enemies). It was here that they had come together to undertake disciplinary action against the tribe of Benjamin after the abuse and murder of a travelling Levite's concubine (see the account in Judges 20 and 21 – not pleasant reading). As already seen, it was also where the nation, or its representatives, had previously congregated to collectively repent and turn back to God before witnessing His miraculous deliverance from the oppressive and overwhelming Philistine military forces.

Samuel had to clearly spell out God's view

It may therefore have been quite reasonable for Mizpah to also be the venue for the new king to be identified and revealed in the public arena. The fact that it was sited in the area allocated to the tribe of Benjamin (Saul's tribe) was probably not a coincidence. However, before any recognition process could commence, Samuel had to clearly spell out (literally – subsequently putting it in writing) God's view of this situation regarding kingship. *'But you have now rejected your God, who saves you out of all your calamities and distresses. And you have said, "No, set a king over us." So now present yourselves before the LORD by your tribes and clans'* (1 Samuel 10:19).

CASTING LOTS

The public selection of Israel's king then commences. The first stage is when the tribe of Benjamin is identified and then, from within that tribe, the clan of Matri (see verse 21). How these respective selections occurred is not described. Past events, such as establishing the culprit responsible for disobeying God's instruction and retaining gold and silver from the ruins of the now-demolished and conquered Jericho, had seen the use of the 'casting of lots' (see Joshua 7:16–18). This was subsequently used by Saul himself, having been appointed king, when he needed to find the soldier who had broken the fast that he'd needlessly instituted. The process revealed this to be his own son, Jonathan (see 1 Samuel 14:41–43).

However, the use of lots was not to be a failsafe method! The Bible records that its track record was less than 100 per cent. The early Church, in seeking a replacement in the apostolic team for the traitor, Judas, made use of lots. Although a man named Matthias was consequently chosen, he was never actually heard of again. Instead it was an entirely unlikely person in the form of Paul (initially named Saul), the arch-enemy of Christians but then dramatically converted, who was clearly God's choice for this position.

THE 'URIM' AND 'THUMMIM'

Back to that selection process. The other means available at that time, although it may have been incorporated in that 'casting of lots', was what was called the *'Urim and Thummim'*. These were possibly precious stones placed in the priestly breastplate and designated as the means by which decisions could be made. *'Whenever Aaron enters the Holy Place, he will bear the names of the sons of Israel over his heart on the breastpiece of decision as a continuing memorial before the LORD. Also put the Urim and the Thummim in the breastpiece, so they may be over Aaron's heart whenever he enters the presence of the LORD. Thus Aaron will always bear the means of making decisions for the Israelites over his heart before the* LORD' (Exodus 28:29−30). David, successor to King Saul, certainly made use of this when having to decide on a course of action in life-or-death situations. The first was when he was on the run and unsure whether to stay put in a town called Keilah which he had relieved from a Philistine terrorist attack. God's reply on that occasion was for him not to hang around. It was repeated when needing to know whether to pursue a band of Amalekite militia who had attacked his camp (in the absence of himself and his soldiers) and carried off wives and children. God directed such a pursuit with a successful interception, resulting in the total rescue of all these potential hostages (see 1 Samuel 23:1−13; 30:1−20).

Whichever of these processes was actually adopted in Saul's case, the end result was public selection of him as Israel's first king. But he was not around when declared the 'winner'! People had to look for him as he was *'not to be found'*. So whatever was done it did not constitute any 'beauty parade' involving a judgement based on physique, demeanour, attire or persona in which he had to participate. This was to the credit of the people and their leaders. It was only after Saul surfaced from the baggage amongst the animals that it was established that *'he was a head taller than any of the others'* (1 Samuel 10:23). His attitude also made a positive mark, it being recorded that he remained silent when troublemakers voiced dissent and doubt over his ability to serve Israel.

Why was Saul hiding when the choice of kingship was made? Perhaps it was genuine reluctance or fearful reticence that kept him in the familiar surroundings of donkeys − his comfort zone. But God knew where he was secreting himself and where he needed to be. The enquiry to God by the people − no doubt including Samuel himself − brought the revelation as to his whereabouts, and he was consequently dragged out into the open, a clear example of 'focusing beyond the horizon' having a very practical application.

MAKING CHOICES

This whole area of choices, decisions and courses of action has caused much concern – and a large number of books written – on the subject of guidance. Perhaps the lack of real options in the past meant that this issue did not have such a high profile. But now, even with financial constraints having to be taken into account, there exists a huge number of possibilities that lie open before us at whatever stage of life. And these relate to almost every facet of life. The options and opportunities may seem endless. Unfortunately there is no heavenly website to provide a link in order for our life's blueprint to be sent as an email attachment!

However, this passage in 1 Samuel 10 does give some positive pointers. 'Focusing' has very practical aspects resulting in keeping our feet on the ground when facing perplexing circumstances and particularly important, life-shaping, decisions like choosing a king! This includes the following:

1. *Step-by-step.* The verses describe a discernible series of sequential actions. Breaking down our choices into bite-sized factors can help clear away aspects that are not relevant and clarify those on which we need to aim.

2. *Setting aside time.* The actual time-scale of events in this account is not revealed. But nobody seemed to be in a hurry apart from when they ran to drag Saul out into the open! Whatever it took to pray and talk through the situation was taken. If at all possible we should not be pressed or hurried into making a decision. This is not to advocate procrastination. It simply

means that if we are required to make quick or panicky choices, more time should be requested. God is not in a hurry and does not want us to be pressured into taking unsuitable directions.

3. *Stillness before God*. This is linked to the time element and is suggested in the chapter by way of asking God whether Saul was around and waiting for an answer. Sometimes we may be asking God the wrong question and therefore not getting a response. Being quiet and waiting for God can be hard work. However, it is necessary in order to hear what He wants to say, whatever means He uses to do so.

4. *Seek God*. Samuel was someone who had God as his priority and followed His revealed way in all situations. The position that he was now facing was no different from all the others in that he consistently talked to God. We cannot switch into 'God-mode' when needing it because of big decisions, and expect Him to respond, whilst the rest of the time doing our 'own thing'.

5. *Surrounded by others*. Whether the people around Samuel were a positive help on this occasion was not clear. They certainly seemed to be making the right noises. But involving prayerful support and advice from those around us is a wise and Biblical step to take.

6. *Stepping out*. We can never be 100 per cent sure of making the right decision, even with hindsight. Theologians have discussed whether Saul could have been the right man all along if he had not 'lost the plot'. Samuel certainly put every effort into steering him in God's ways and had initially seemed **Saul lost the plot** certain that he was the 'right man for the job', acting on what he believed God had said. But whatever the stage in making choices, there is always going to be an element of 'stepping out'. We will need to get close to God

and trust Him for the consequences, believing that He can redeem every situation.

7. *Speak to God.* Pray and keep on praying. Samuel was a man of prayer. He pointed this out to the nation in his 'farewell speech': *'As for me, far be it from me that I should sin against the* LORD *by failing to pray for you'* (1 Samuel 12:23). He is also specified in the Psalms in that way: *'Samuel was among those who called on his name; they called on the* LORD*'* (Psalm 99:6). The answers and direction we need from God come when we are on our knees . . . the place where our focus goes beyond our present situations.

FOR REFLECTION:

- Why do you think it was necessary for God to instigate, through Samuel, this step-by-step approach in identifying Saul as king?
- How do you feel that such an approach in dealing with perplexing circumstances and difficult decisions can help us focus and trust in God?
- Why do you feel that there is often a time factor involved in sensing God's response to our requests for help in making decisions?
- Why was prayer such a vital element in Samuel's life, and particularly in this situation?

Our response: Think about a specific decision that you are needing to make, either now or in the near future, and then write down the different steps you feel are appropriate in order to make it.

8

KEEPING TO
THE GAME-PLAN

But Samuel replied: '. . . To obey is better than sacrifice . . .'
(1 Samuel 15:22)

READING: 1 SAMUEL 13:1–15; 15:1–15

The directions on the sheet were quite explicit: 'Read all this leaflet carefully before you use these eye drops.' The nurse who handed me the prescribed medication underlined some of the crucial points that needed to be remembered. To ensure the best outcome in terms of rectified vision, I needed to do what I was told! And no questions asked! Spiritual 'vision' requires the same kind of response.

In sport a similar approach makes use of the phrase 'game-plan'. It refers to the outcome of intensive and careful study by coaches, trainers, skills-technicians and managers to ensure that their team players achieve an end-goal, success! As with a healthcare scenario, each member of the side has to take this on board to fulfil the plan.

These closing chapters of 1 Samuel are mainly concerned with Saul, the first appointed king of Israel. But his actions and responses to events are intertwined and contrasted with those of the *'seer'*, Samuel.

It is noticeable that Samuel's ability to see and know what God is doing is linked with his ready obedience. He was always keeping to God's 'game-plan'. And he did his best to stress the importance of doing so to the nation. In what might be termed his 'farewell speech,' stepping down as their Judge-Leader, his final rallying cry underlined this point: *'Be sure to fear the LORD and serve him faithfully with all your heart; consider what great things he has done for you. Yet if you persist in doing evil, both you and your king will be swept away'* (1 Samuel 12:24–25). Sadly, his concerns were to prove well-founded.

A GOOD START

As time progressed we find that Saul failed to keep to God's 'game-plan'. His leadership had, however, started in an extremely positive way. The town of Jabesh-Gilead, situated on the east of the Jordan River in the tribal area of Manasseh, was besieged by Nahash and his forces belonging to the Ammonite people-group (who were related to the Israelites, descended from Abraham's nephew, Lot).

When Saul heard of this attack and the harsh conditions of surrender that had been imposed (gouging out every citizen's right eye – definitely not included in the Geneva Convention!), he was prompted to act. *'The Spirit of God came upon him in power'* (1 Samuel 11:6). His rallying cry, backed up with stern consequences for those who failed to respond, resulted in a large army being assembled. Their pre-dawn attack on the Ammonites resulted in victorious annihilation of the enemy. Reaffirmation of Saul's kingship followed this success at the instigation of Samuel (see 1 Samuel 11:12–13).

DUEL LEADERSHIP

But was Saul's leadership to be undertaken alone? There are strong indications that, although he was to be the king, this role was to be carried out in harness with Samuel as spiritual leader. That national challenge to respond to the threat of the Ammonites had been graphic and instructive as far as the leadership structure was concerned. *'He* [Saul] *took a pair of oxen, cut them into pieces, and sent the pieces by messengers throughout Israel proclaiming: "This is what will be done to the oxen of anyone who does not follow Saul and Samuel"'* (1 Samuel 11:7).

However, somewhere along the line, Saul lost the plot. His leadership alongside Samuel was clearly to be under God's control. Confirmation of his position had been confirmed *'in the presence of the* LORD', with offerings being sacrificed *'before the* LORD', as a way of emphasising this vital element (11:15).

THE PHILISTINES ATTACK

The first hint that Saul had started to follow his own agenda came when the Philistine threat re-emerged. His focus at that time was definitely not beyond the horizon. Instead, all he could see was the massed formations of chariots and soldiers that now opposed him in response to his son's attacks on one of the Philistine outposts. The rank and file of Saul's army also saw these forces . . . and voted with their feet! *'When the men of Israel saw that their situation was critical and that their army was hard pressed, they hid in caves and thickets, among the rocks, and in pits and cisterns'* (1 Samuel 13:6). But there was worse to come. *'Some Hebrews even crossed the Jordan to the land of Gad and Gilead'* (verse 7). Not a promising scenario!

Even the soldiers who stuck with Saul were *'quaking with fear'*, before they also *'began to scatter'*. Lack of military hardware was also a factor. It was recorded: *'Not a blacksmith could be found in the whole land of Israel'* (verse 19). This was on account of the Philistines who had somehow manipulated resources so that they alone could provide a service for sharpening and fashioning essential agricultural and domestic tools. Only Saul and his son Jonathan actually possessed any fighting gear.

SAMUEL'S INSTRUCTIONS . . .

It may be asked why Saul had not launched a pre-emptive attack whilst his forces were still able to act cohesively and before mounting fear completely overwhelmed them. The answer to Saul's inactivity is found by referring back possibly three years to that very first early-morning briefing from Samuel. Included in all that data was foreknowledge of a pivotal event. *'After that you will go to Gibeah of God, where there is a Philistine outpost . . . Go down ahead of me to Gilgal. I will surely come down to you to sacrifice burnt offerings and fellowship offerings, but you must wait seven days until I come to you and tell you what you are to do'* (1 Samuel 10:5, 8).

. . . AND SAUL'S FAILURE TO WAIT

The fulfilment of Samuel's prophecy had now arrived. Saul, at this critical stage, stood on the threshold of vast possibilities which involved two things. First, whether he was prepared to act as God's vice-regent through the instruction of Samuel, and not as absolute monarch pursuing his own agenda. Secondly, and linked to this, whether he could control his impetuous nature and impulses. Both of these involved focusing beyond himself and his perceived horizon. He almost achieved it. Up until almost the last moment he waited. But Samuel had still not appeared after that seven-day designated period.

Saul held back until possibly within half an hour (because to offer a burnt offering and a peace offering could not take much longer). He then stepped over that invisible line. *'So he said, "Bring me the burnt offering and the fellowship offerings." And Saul offered up the burnt offering'* (1 Samuel 13:9). The next verse comes with a sense of foreboding. *'Just as he finished making the offering, Samuel arrived'* (verse 10). The resultant conversation is brief . . . and pointed. Saul's lame explanation for acting unilaterally and outside his responsibility (he was not charged with the priestly role of offering sacrifices – that was Samuel's task as part of the game-plan) was met with an irreversible rebuke: *'You acted foolishly . . . But now your kingdom will not endure'* (1 Samuel 13:13, 14).

Samuel acted in accordance with God's 'game-plan'. Saul did not. The lesson that comes with considerable force is that the person who wants to follow God and focus beyond the horizon to see what is really happening must also be one who obeys and waits for God. This may mean having to stand in a place of chaos, diminishing hope and **obeys and** no way out. The Old Testament prophet **waits for God** Jeremiah was in such a place. When fleeing from occupied Jerusalem with other Jews, he was approached by his compatriots. They wanted to know if their proposed course of action of heading for Egypt was right. Having asked the question they, and Jeremiah, had to wait for God's response . . . which took days (and *we* complain if our emails don't arrive in a split second). *'Ten days later the word of the LORD came to Jeremiah'* (Jeremiah 42:7).

FURTHER FAILURE

But worse was to come. Samuel's ability to focus on God's ways is again linked to his readiness to act on what He said. He promptly brings a message from *'the LORD Almighty'* to the king (1 Samuel 15:2). This is in respect of the Amalekite people-group (descended from Esau, Jacob's twin brother) who, God decrees, are now to be punished for their attack on the Israelites as they escaped from Egypt (see Deuteronomy 25:17–19).

However, Saul again fails. His attack and victory result in the capture of the Amalekite king. But the instruction to '*put to death men and women, children and infants, cattle and sheep, camels and donkeys*' (1 Samuel 15:3) is not completely carried out. Along with their king, the best of the livestock is spared. When Samuel is told by God of this failure we read: '*Samuel was troubled, and he cried out to the LORD all that night*' (15:11). However, he knows what he has to do and, promptly next morning, he confronts Saul. Pointing out to him that obedience to God is more important than religious activity, he then slays the captured leader . . . and informs Saul that he has been rejected as king over Israel.

LOOKING AT OTHERS

Once again Saul had taken notice of what other people around him had been doing and wanting, rather than focusing on the ways of the Lord. God's requirement had been clear. Saul, however, chose to turn a blind eye to his troops' failure to act on them. His poor excuse to Samuel when confronted with this disobedience put the onus on others: '*The soldiers brought them from the Amalakites; they spared the best of the sheep and cattle to sacrifice to the LORD your God, but we totally destroyed the rest*' (15:14–15). It was noticeable that there was no sign of genuine repentance or seeking of forgiveness by Saul in respect of either failure.

Revelation from God – being given spiritual insight into what is taking place beyond our normal understanding – comes from being fully submitted and obedient to Him. It is a consistent feature of the Old Testament prophets that they acted on what God told them even though it might not have made sense or was risky. Even Jonah came to that painful conclusion having spent three days in a very unpleasant environment following his unwise decision to go AWOL!

Thus Samuel and Saul left each other at the end of this episode. We are told: *'Until the day Samuel died, he did not go to see Saul again, though Samuel mourned for him'* (1 Samuel 15:35). However on account of continuing obedience to God he was given further revelation and insight. He was instructed to anoint Israel's next king, *'a man after his* [God's] *own heart'* (13:14). Meanwhile Saul, choosing to go his own way rather than God's, ended his days in fear, failure and defeat.

FOR REFLECTION:

- What possible reasons caused Saul to act outside the instructions that had been given through Samuel on those two occasions when confronting Israel's enemies?
- How explicit had been those instructions regarding what he was to do?
- What was the difference in outcome for Saul between those two occasions when he failed to follow instructions?
- Why do you feel that it was important for Saul, and important for us, to take on board what God says so that we may then be able to 'focus beyond the horizon'?

Our response: Write down some direction which you believe God has given or underlined for you, but which you are not finding easy to follow.

9

EXPECTATIONS

Then the LORD said: 'Rise and anoint him; he is the one.'
(1 Samuel 16:12)

READING: 1 SAMUEL 16:1–13

The world's first jet airliner was the British-built *De Havilland Comet*. It was the forerunner of the Airbuses, Jumbo Jets and Dreamliners that now effortlessly whisk sun-seekers and business managers around the globe. The *Comet*'s maiden flight was back in 1949 and it entered passenger-carrying service four years later – a world beater at that time. It was a quantum leap forward in technology and performance, epitomised by its sleek lines and silver finish. But its designers failed to appreciate the stresses that its considerably higher speed and flying altitude would have on its structure. Their expectations were based on previous experience and current aeronautical knowledge.

However the subsequent catastrophic in-flight disintegration of three Comets in separate incidents between 1953 and 1954 caused the whole fleet to be grounded. Intensive investigations were undertaken to determine the cause of these successive crashes. This included salvaging the shattered remains of one of these aircraft from the depths of the Mediterranean Sea. The engineers discovered that unanticipated strains had caused metal fatigue to develop in the pressurised cabin fuselage, resulting in the aircraft breaking up. A new, safe, *Comet* design eventually emerged based on these findings. But by that time the American aircraft industry had capitalised on this necessary research into aerodynamic stresses and taken the lead in civil aviation. Fifty years of flight had led to certain expectations, but changes now rendered these inapplicable, and new designs were needed.

FURTHER INSTRUCTIONS

We have been looking at some aspects of 'focusing beyond the horizon' and how these applied to the life of Samuel, the prophet and Judge. Contrasted with Saul, his submissive and undistracted attitude towards God enabled him to have an understanding of situations that was not immediately obvious – a God-perspective. But there is at least one more factor to be noted. This arises through Samuel receiving further instructions from God. As on previous occasions he responds promptly . . . and heads for Bethlehem.

However, circumstances have now changed considerably, and Samuel makes this journey with very mixed emotions. On the one hand he is grieving deeply at the plight of Saul whose disobedience of God's clear command had resulted in severe consequences. God had to address Samuel's reaction quite firmly: *'How long will you mourn for Saul, since I have rejected him as king over Israel?'* (1 Samuel 16:1). But then God points to a new hope. *'Fill your horn with oil and be on your way; I am sending*

God points to a new hope

you to Jesse of Bethlehem. I have chosen one of his sons to be king.' This gives rise to Samuel's second emotion, fear. Saul was developing a paranoia about his status and felt threatened. So Samuel asks God, *'How can I go? Saul will hear about it and kill me.'* God's response that he was to go on the pretext of making a *'sacrifice to the LORD'* may have subdued his fears, but not those of the inhabitants of his destination. They were decidedly edgy! *'The elders of the town trembled when they met him. They asked, "Do you come in peace?"'* (1 Samuel 16:4). Samuel's assurance opened the way for the next stage of God's plan.

AN IMPORTANT LESSON

But things now get interesting! God had said to Samuel that Jesse and his sons were to be invited to this sacrifice and that He would show him what to do. Responding to this invitation, Jesse accordingly summons seven of his sons to this event. It is at this point that Samuel learns an important lesson. God was not to be bound by the ways in which He had worked in the past, or what He had done previously. Just like those aircraft designers, things might look similar, but something new and different was about to take place.

One of Jesse's sons was to be the new king. But which one? Saul, Israel's first king, had been specifically recorded as being *'a head taller than any of the others'*, and it was said that, *'There is no-one like him among all the people'* (1 Samuel 10:23, 24). Working on that premise, Samuel viewed Jesse's first son, Eliab. When he did so he thought, *'Surely the LORD'S anointed stands here before the LORD'* (1 Samuel 16:6). Acting on what he considered the criteria for choosing a king – appearance and height – Samuel had been anticipating a divine 'stamp of approval'. He was in for a big shock!

God's response was categorical! *'Do not consider his appearance or his height, for I have rejected him. The LORD does not look at the things man looks at. Man looks at the outward appearance, but the LORD looks at the heart'* (1 Samuel 16:7).

THE YOUNGEST

God's rebuff to Samuel's proposition may seem harsh. However, it was necessary in order to help him understand that insight is not static, but needs to deepen. There is always more of God for us to know by his Holy Spirit. Thus it was that Samuel, having each of Jesse's sons pass by him and be rejected by God, asked (with possible desperation!) if, actually, there were any more sons around. The response, *'There is still the youngest'* (16:11), was possibly met with an inward sigh of relief by the prophet.

Samuel perhaps wasn't listening to Jesse's dismissive comment that this unnamed, youngest son had not been summoned on account of *'tending the sheep'*. All that he needed to know was that there was another son. The interval between Samuel's instruction to *'Send for him'* and his eventual arrival may have been a lengthy one. Perhaps it gave necessary time for Samuel to digest what all of us need to learn – God operates outside our parameters, criteria and expectations.

The way that God looks at people is seen in the dealings that Jesus had with those around Him. He chose twelve disciples whom others had written-off as being sub-standard material for a Jewish rabbi to mentor. He was the *'friend'* of tax-collectors and other *'sinners'*. He went out of His way to meet a five-times married Samaritan woman now cohabiting. He approached *'unclean'* lepers, responded to beggars, crossed a stormy lake to bring deliverance to a demon-oppressed maniac. He saw the unnoticed widow placing two small-value coins into the temple collection.

All the time He saw, within people's hearts, a desperation for God to intervene.

So it was that David, considered too young and unsuitable by outward standards, was the man chosen by God to be the next and greatest king of Israel. He was also to be the human ancestor of the King of kings and Saviour of the world. But his anointing into that role only came about because Samuel needed to learn to expect more of God, not assessing on the basis of what had happened previously.

Just as the choice of David as king was derived in a different way from that of Saul, so too was the effect of the symbolic anointing with oil. In Saul's case we read that God's Spirit only came upon him later. But with David the Spirit of the Lord came upon him in power *'from that day on'* (1 Samuel 16:13). It is interesting to note that this was the same experience that Jesus subsequently had at the time of His water baptism – Jesus being described as David's 'greater son'. Connected with that is the fact that John the Baptist, who performed this baptism, was the last of the prophets, whilst Samuel (who anointed David) was the first.

FOLLOWING GOD'S INSTRUCTIONS

David himself was to show awareness of the fact that God works in ways outside our expectation or previous experience. Many years later, after he had been given the kingship of Israel, those perennial enemies, the Philistines, again emerged to threaten his nascent reign. *'When the Philistines heard that David had been anointed king over Israel, they went up in full force to search for him'* (2 Samuel 5:17). David then turned to God, who told him, *'Go, for I will surely hand the Philistines over to you'* (verse 19). Following David's subsequent victory we find that the threat returns. Those Philistines were gluttons for punishment . . . or simply plain stupid! Once more David goes to God. He may have anticipated a similar response. Instead God instructed him to adopt different tactics. *'Do not go straight up, but circle round behind them and attack them in front of the balsam trees. As soon as you hear the sound of marching in the tops of the balsam trees, move quickly, because that will mean the LORD has gone out in front of you to strike the Philistine army'* (2 Samuel 5:23–24). The word from God was different – but the outcome was the same! *'So David did as the LORD commanded him, and he struck down the Philistines all the way from Gibeon to Gezer'* (verse 25).

As Christians living in a very secular age, it is easy for us to be caught up in the ways of the world that we see around us. This means that we can slip into the practices and attitudes of those who have no thought or regard for God. As a consequence we act, very largely, on the grounds of what we see and know, together with accumulated experience of what God has done in the past. This has also been the case with churches which have been founded on a particular move of God or teaching, but then found themselves stuck in tradition and denominational practices.

SOMETHING PRACTICAL

But God wants our focus to be on Him all the time and not to rely on either human judgement or a particular past experience of Him. Sometimes this can have a very down-to-earth application . . . like buying a house! This was my ordeal some time ago, before the age of 'virtual' viewing or advertising of properties on websites. Needing to move on and not finding anywhere suitable to rent, it seemed that this was God's indication that I should look to actually buy a place. But again there seemed nothing that felt 'right', despite having registered with several estate agents who forwarded information on flats that ticked at least some of the right 'boxes'. So again, feeling that God was 'steering' me in the direction of a house instead (the economics of which was decidedly 'going out on a limb'), I took the normal steps to see what was around. Again a blank was drawn.

Finally, sharing all of this with my church leaders, they made the suggestion that I . . . get on my bike! To be more precise, I should cycle around the area where I believed God wanted me to live (given constraints of church and work involvement, together with family connections) and note the houses which displayed 'For Sale' boards outside. This information could then be used to check price and house details, together with praying about them. This was definitely not a scheme laid down in any house-buyer's guide. But God had an even better idea! This was evident when, on the allotted late afternoon, I was following through on that suggestion. However, when cycling down one of the roads in the area, I saw a friend from my previous church who was cycling in the road ahead. Stopping to chat, he asked what I was doing. As I explained my unusual house-seeking efforts he responded by saying that his house (in that area) was going up for sale, although as yet it had no sign to show that fact, and would I like to have a look? I most certainly did . . . the house that I subsequently bought and in which I have been living since that time.

Whatever challenges we may be encountering, such as in the areas of guidance, healing, relationship or provision, it may be that God wants us to see something different in terms of how He is working. Let's have our spiritual insight focused beyond the horizon in expectation of Him doing something new.

FOR REFLECTION:

- Why do you feel that we generally find it easier to stay with the familiar and normal rather than going for something untried and untested?
- What specific steps of faith can you identify Samuel needing to take as this account takes us through to the eventual anointing of David?
- Why was God saying to Samuel that it was more important to see the heart of a person rather than their physical appearance?
- What was it that marked out David (see also 1 Samuel 16:18)?

Our response: Think about an area of your life where you are needing, or will need, to make a choice, and write down the different factors which could determine which direction you might take. Mark out those which might be vital but not so obvious.

10

BEYOND THIS
HORIZON

Immediately Saul fell full length on the ground,
filled with fear because of Samuel's words.
(1 Samuel 28:20)

READING: 1 SAMUEL 28:3–25

He was a sceptic. He was also an advertising agent. Perhaps these two facts were linked! But he was also a writer and set out to analyse the sources relating to what he considered to be the myth of Jesus' resurrection. His short paper was intended to present these findings. However, this did not develop as planned. As he compiled his material he became convinced of the fact of this miracle. The book that Frank Morison (his pseudonym) wrote in 1930 was entitled *Who Moved the Stone?* Many have read this reasoned account and have subsequently also become Christians.

However, the resurrection of Jesus is not the only account in the Bible of a return from death. Other interventions from God to bring people back to this life are also described. They all point to the almighty power of God and Jesus' sin-defeating death on the Cross and hell-beating resurrection. Because of what Jesus had done, attested by the Biblical writers and affirmed by that twentieth-century sceptic-turned-believer, the apostle Paul could exclaim: *'Where, O death, is your victory? Where, O death, is your sting?'* (1 Corinthians 15:55).

BACK TO LIFE

The Gospel accounts record Jesus bringing three people back to life. These were Lazarus His friend (John 11), Jairus' daughter (Luke 8:41–56) and the widow of Nain's son (Luke 7:11–13). But the New Testament is not alone in showing God's power in this way. The Old Testament prophets Elijah and Elisha are also described as being used by God to raise people from the dead. And there is also Samuel. His account is somewhat obscure and gets little coverage from commentators or preachers! That's possibly because it is not an 'ordinary' raising from the dead – is there any that is ordinary? Although it raises awkward questions, it also presents some encouragements . . . which point us beyond this horizon!

The background to this narrative concerning Samuel again brings us to those Philistines. They had assembled their military forces against the Israelites in a further scheme to defeat and destroy God's people. King Saul's response is to gather an army. But when he saw what he was up against, *'he was afraid; terror filled his heart'* (1 Samuel 28:5). This reaction was compounded by the fact that he was alone. Earlier in that chapter it is stated: *'Now Samuel was dead, and all Israel had mourned for him and buried him in his own town of Ramah'* (verse 3). Not only did Saul have no-one to bring a Godly perspective and power to bear on this devastating prospect, but God Himself was not responding: *'He enquired of the LORD, but the LORD did not answer him by dreams or Urim or prophets'* (verse 6).

A 'NO-GO' AREA

Desperate to know what he should do and what the outcome will be, Saul resorts to spiritism. He commands his attendants: *'Find me a woman who is a medium, so that I may go and enquire of her'* (1 Samuel 28:7). It was known that there was such a person who was located in Endor. However, this was behind enemy lines and explains, in part, why Saul disguises himself. But not only does he need to venture into unfriendly territory undetected, he also needs to remain anonymous to this spiritist. She, however, is reluctant to *'consult a spirit'* for him as she is aware that the king had expelled all the mediums from the land (see verses 3, 9). This had been in accordance with Mosaic Law (laid down in Leviticus 19:26). All forms of spiritism and associated activity were, and continue to be, a definite no-go area for God's people. True repentance towards God includes dealing drastically with all associated artefacts such as the Ephesian Christians owned and consequentially burnt, thereby losing a huge amount of money (see Acts 19:13–19).

THE RULER OVER ALL

In that spiritually and physically darkened atmosphere the medium, assured of immunity, asks who it is that Saul wants to be brought up. His answer is brief . . . and awesome: *'Bring up Samuel'* (verse 11). This is the point of encouragement . . . Samuel is, indeed, 'brought up' but not because of any spiritist activity by that woman, but solely by the power of God Almighty. Her response at the appearance of Samuel was sheer terror! This was not on her agenda. Deceiving spirits and fraudulent demons pretending to be departed people, yes; but the resurrection of a dead person, no! Her next response – accusing Saul of tricking her – smacks of the 'kettle calling the pot black'. This account

He rules over all powers

highlights that God is not restricted by death, sickness, hell or Satan. He rules over all powers, seen and unseen. Of God's Son Jesus it is categorically stated: *'He is the image of the invisible God, the firstborn over all creation. For by him all things were created: things in heaven and on earth, visible and invisible, whether thrones or powers or rulers or authorities; all things were created by him and for him. He is before all things, and in him all things hold together. And he is the head of the body, the church; he is the beginning and the firstborn from among the dead, so that in everything he might have the supremacy'* (Colossians 1:15–18).

The power of Jesus was clearly demonstrated in His time on earth when He consistently took authority over, and expelled from people's bodies, Satanic spirits hell-bent on stealing, killing and destroying lives (see such deliverances described in Matthew 8:28–34; 9:32–33; 12:22; 15:21–28; 17:14–18). The authority that Jesus then delegated to His disciples added substance to the fact that He had such power in the spiritual realm in the first place. *'The seventy-two returned with joy and said, "Lord, even the demons submit to us in your name"'* (Luke 10:17). Mark's Gospel brings this up to date, showing that our focus is to be beyond the horizon by means of this authority: *'And these signs will accompany those who believe: In my name they will drive out demons; they will speak in new tongues; they will pick up snakes with their hands; and when they drink deadly poison, it will not hurt them at all; they will place their hands on sick people, and they will get well'* (Mark 16:17–18).

However, it doesn't seem that Samuel is very impressed with being brought back to an earthly environment, asking Saul the question: *'Why have you disturbed me by bringing me up?'* (1 Samuel 28:15). Saul's answer, describing his terrible plight and lack of response from God, is met with a stern reply reminding him that these events were what Samuel had previously predicted. But then he adds a shocking pronouncement: *'The LORD will hand over both Israel and you to the Philistines, and tomorrow you and your sons will be with me. The LORD will also hand over the army of Israel to the Philistines'* (verse 19).

ONE LAST 'FOCUS'

Samuel was 'focusing beyond the horizon' for one last time with that pronouncement, telling Saul what was to take place within the next 24 hours. In doing so, this was actually an act of mercy towards Saul, and another encouragement for us. For Saul it meant that there was yet time to repent. His imminent death was the specific result of his disobedience; this had led to God's rejection of his kingship. Although he had shown regret and remorse at that time, there had been no true repentance.

But now there is one last opportunity to turn back to God, acknowledging his failure and asking forgiveness. The outcome of the forthcoming battle may not be different, but that was to be a mere blip in comparison to eternity that was to follow and on which Saul's response hinged.

one last opportunity

The good news is that God's heart is that none should perish (see 2 Peter 3:9). For this reason every person may, in some form or other, be offered the opportunity to repent. This may be even within moments of departing from this life, as Saul was to experience. It is said that of the two thieves on the cross, alongside Jesus at His crucifixion, one was saved so that all may have hope, but only one lest any presume that all will automatically be saved without true repentance.

BEYOND THIS LIFE

The final encouragement from this sombre scene is that it is a reminder of the fact that our lives are not in the hands of fate or circumstances, or the whims of chance, or even other people. Rather, our lives are in the hands of God. The psalmist described it in this way: *'All the days ordained for me were written in your book before one of them came to be'* (Psalm 139:16). Samuel was able to tell Saul that his time in this life was very soon to be finished. This was not an isolated example. The prophet Isaiah brought God's message to King Hezekiah many years after Saul, telling him to *'put his house in order'* on account of his impending death from illness (see 2 Kings 20:1). The king's response, one of turning to God in desperate and heartfelt prayer (contrasting with Saul's absence of such contrition), resulted in an adjustment to that date . . . it was moved back 15 years!

God has the power and authority to make such a statement and subsequently change it! This whole scenario raises questions to which we have no proper answers. With our limited understanding we have to accept many of these aspects of God on trust. We will not know the full picture until we reach Glory . . . and then may find our questions to be irrelevant! But it highlights the fact that, like Abraham, who was described as *'looking forward to the city with foundations, whose architect and builder is God'* (Hebrews 11:10), we too are called by faith to 'focus beyond the horizon' of this life to our real home and destiny.

FOR REFLECTION:

- Why does God not want us to have any involvement in forms of spiritism such as Tarot cards, horoscopes and Ouija boards?
- Why was Saul in such a state of terror and fear?
- What comfort can we draw from the fact that Jesus has total authority over every power of our spiritual enemy and his devices such as sickness and death?
- What reassurance can we know in remembering that God has numbered our days?

Our response: Write down two things which you can do in order to focus more on eternal life that is to come, spent in heaven, rather than getting too strongly attached to the things of this life.

APPENDIX

OTHERS WHO FOCUSED

One of the problems in reading about the 'high profile' people in the Bible is that we tend to feel distant from them. Rather like our contemporary sporting or media celebrities, they seem to live in a different world from our own. We can follow such contemporaries on Twitter and Facebook, but cannot genuinely connect with them. At one level this is true with those Biblical characters. Their culture, geographical location and era are far removed from our present-day experience . . . though missing out on our 'social media' is probably something they wouldn't have regretted!!

In a spiritual sense they also appear to be on a very different level. Samuel may especially be viewed in this light. We've seen him rubbing shoulders with the 'great and the good' (and the not-so-good), directing military actions and speaking to the nation. This is not where most of us are at! He also seems to have a 'hotline' to God . . . who doesn't fob him off with a voicemail message.

But as we have seen, being close to God and having understanding of people and situations beyond our natural knowledge and insight did not 'just happen'. The basis of what was taking place included Samuel's submission and obedience to God, together with prayerful listening. These helped put him in a position to 'focus beyond the horizon'. Such actions, whatever events were taking place around him, are also within our grasp with God's help.

But was Samuel the only one whose example we can emulate? Clearly there are such people, and not only those who hit the headlines. Which is why the handful of examples sketched in this Appendix may be helpful. They consist of lesser known and almost obscure people. They are men and women with whom we can more easily identify. Like us, they were getting on with life away from the limelight, occupying their days with the routine and nondescript. They knew what it was to be under pressure and carry responsibilities. However, they all, in some way, showed that it was still possible to focus outside their current circumstances, and step out to see a horizon beyond . . . as we can, taking on board some of the lessons that they show us.

DAUGHTERS OF ZELOPHEHAD – GOING OUT ON A LIMB

Give us property among our father's relatives.
(Numbers 27:4)

It was a strange request. To our ears it was positively weird. But even to those at the time it was baffling. So much so that a second opinion was needed . . . God's. What was it that was being asked? More to the point, who was asking it? And what was the motive?

Hidden away in the Old Testament book of Numbers is an

account of a conversation. It's between five young women and a venerable old man. His identity is familiar to us. This is Moses, the leader of the Children of Israel, whom God used to enable His people to escape from Egyptian slavery. Having achieved that exodus they travel through the desert, aiming for the Promised Land. A journey that should take eleven days is made to take slightly longer – 40 years to be precise! This was because of the Israelites' unbelief at God's promised provision of that territory, occupied at that time by seemingly immoveable, anti-God inhabitants.

It is as the Children of Israel are eventually within sight of the 'finishing tape' that we read of some women, 'daughters of Zelophehad', approaching Moses. They come with a request: *'Why should our father's name disappear from his clan because he had no son? Give us property among our father's relatives'* (Numbers 27:4). Their names are Mahlah, Tirzah, Hoglah, Milcah and Noah (yes, the female version).

In understanding what was being asked and its significance, we need to be aware of the material and spiritual value of land ownership at that time. In an almost entirely agricultural economy it was not only the source of income but of life itself. Everything depended on its full and successful usage. It was therefore integral to family life and needed to be maintained by succeeding generations. But it was also viewed as a responsibility before God. It was He who was to give them the land in the first place (see Joshua 1:3), and their retention of it, allotted into tribal, clan and family groupings, acted as a recognition of God's Lordship over His people.

This was now at stake. In cultural terms the sons of the family received the land from their fathers and passed it on to their sons. But here was a very simple problem: Zelophehad had no sons. He only (dare that word be used!) had daughters. But what daughters! They saw that the loss of their father's land on account of their gender was not only bad news for themselves, but it did not reflect the heart of God. In that regard they were focusing well beyond the horizon of the cultural mores and practices of their day.

Unfortunately Moses was not so well focused. At least not in this matter. Nor was Eleazar the priest, the leaders, or the whole assembly (see Numbers 27:2). They were all caught off balance by this request: for women to take on the material and spiritual responsibility of land previously shouldered by men. To his credit Moses did not immediately veto the idea. The very fact that these women could approach him to make such a request is a testament to the access that women had in that environment. But it was still, very definitely, going out on a limb and against accepted practice and thought.

The fact that these daughters of Zelophehad were 'focusing beyond the horizon' to grasp what was God's intended purpose, as contrasted with the ideas of Moses and other leaders, was evidenced by God's reply. *'So Moses brought their case before the LORD and the LORD said to him: "What Zelophehad's daughters are saying is right"'* (Numbers 27:6–7). He then confirmed: *'You must certainly give them property as an inheritance among their father's relatives and give their father's inheritance over to them.'* This direction from God gave rise to a ruling on future, similar occurrences described in the subsequent verses (verses 8–11).

Back to those daughters. Their readiness to approach Moses was based on other insights. Firstly they recognised that although their father was not faultless, being one of the generation that died in the wilderness on account of unbelief in God's ability to give them the Promised Land, his sin was not open defiance. That had been the failing of a compatriot named Korah who had headed up a group of Israelites in disputing Moses' right as leader. He received a Divine rebuff and summary dispatch from this life (see Numbers 16:1–34). Zelophehad, by contrast, had *'died for his own sin'*, and not on account of this other wickedness.

Further, these daughters actually believed in and wanted to enter the Promised Land and their inherited provision. They were prepared to step out to ensure that this took place. This was more than some of their tribal members were looking to undertake. Half of their tribe of Manasseh had elected to remain on the east side of the Jordan River rather than engage in contesting the occupation of that territory. The example of these women is to encourage us to view beyond accepted horizons and go out on a limb. We are to be sensitive to God's inspiration and instruction so that we may lay hold of the inheritance which God has for us, individually and as churches, whatever others may think is appropriate.

How great is your goodness, which you have stored up for those who fear you, which you bestow in the sight of men on those who take refuge in you.
(Psalm 31:19)

A YOUNG GIRL – BEING ALERT

He would cure him of his leprosy.
(2 Kings 5:3)

Opportunities come to us in many and mainly unexpected ways. Which is a problem, because recognising them requires alertness and sensitivity . . . most of us struggle in that area! For Christians, many of these opportunities may be about focusing beyond the horizon. This can be a problem! Working in a government department that had ongoing contact with the public, I had not always seen opportunities for God to work. Then the 'penny dropped'! Despite the stress in clearing caseloads and achieving targets, I realised that there was a spiritual element that could be grasped. This was in respect of praying *for* (although not *with*, since that was not feasible) members of the public whom I sensed were in particular need. So, returning home, I would pray for such people although knowing little about their circumstances. I would be very unlikely to know the outcome to such intercession, but it was a means of 'pushing boundaries' in trying to pick up from God on how best to pray for these individuals.

Backtracking around three thousand years, we come to someone else in a difficult work environment. But this is many times worse than dealing with demanding customers and figure-crunching managers in an office. Probably the only similarity is that this girl, whose account is described in 2 Kings 5, was also a cypher, a non-entity – someone whose value and worth was not reckoned to amount to much. She didn't even have a 'zero-hours' contract, let alone get paid a minimum wage. That's because she had been literally plucked from obscurity . . . and put back again, though in a different setting as a slave (to all intents and purposes). She had been *'taken captive'* by an Aramean raiding party who had gone over the border into Israel. This was part of a regular military incursion, the outcome of friction between these two neighbouring states.

This girl was described as one who *'served Naaman's wife'* (2 Kings 5:2). She also served the Living God. As a result of the latter, her obscurity and worthless status were not the factors that shaped her life and focus. Nor is it yours or mine . . . whatever society, our employer, school teachers, even family, may suggest.

It will always be the care and value that God places on us that denotes our true worth.

This servant girl saw something beyond what others could see. Despite having no material resources, academic qualifications or social standing, she saw something that was possible . . . where everyone else saw only a problem. The latter was stated in stark terms regarding her master: *'Now Naaman was commander of the army of the king of Aram. He was a great man in the sight of his master and highly regarded because through him the* LORD *had given victory to Aram. He was a valiant soldier, but he had leprosy'* (2 Kings 5:1).

Naaman was the husband of this girl's mistress and employer. Perhaps she had learnt of his condition before the information went 'public'. However much Naaman might have wanted to hide this disease, he was fighting, for once, a losing battle. However, it seems clear that although he was a successful military commander, with the force of character that entailed, he was still liked by those around him. His servants were subsequently to address him as *'My father'*, and to vigorously persuade him to act in accordance with what the prophet Elisha was to direct when his initial response had been to refuse. But we've jumped ahead. Naaman first had to learn of the existence of God's prophet and the power that was working through him. This was where the girl came centre stage. She, like those servants, indicated some feeling towards Naaman and his plight. She also knew God and His capability. Thus she 'focused beyond the horizon' in declaring not only the fact that the prophet was in Samaria but that, *'He would cure him of his leprosy'* (2 Kings 5:3).

This girl not only seized an opportunity to declare the power of God, but also stated that this would be effective in the life of someone who was not one of His chosen people. This was an amazing insight. Centuries later Jesus Himself underlined that point at the beginning of his ministry when He read from Isaiah 61 in the synagogue. He reminded his hearers that God's favour was not for the Jews alone. A Gentile woman from Zarephath, and this Syrian commander Naaman, were both recipients of God's touch through, respectively, the prophets Elijah and Elisha (see Luke 4:16–30). This did not win Him any popularity points! But it was a truth that was first 'seen' by this girl.

Not only did this girl have this understanding that God was working outside accepted national and ethnic boundaries, but she also saw that He was able to work in a way not previously experienced. This is the first mention of the dreaded disease of leprosy being tackled head-on. The Red Sea had been crossed, Jericho's walls had disintegrated, the sun's orbit stopped, and the dead brought back to life as demonstrations of God's power. The girl no doubt knew of these mighty acts. But leprosy . . .? Do you or I have a seemingly unique and unsolvable problem to which no-one else has seen an answer from God? The words of this girl are testimony to the fact that nothing is impossible with God.

Whether we identify with the girl's status, or the problem, we can see that neither situation is a barrier to focusing beyond the horizon to see God's power, if only we would first be alert to the opportunity that our circumstances present.

JONATHAN – FORCEFULLY ADVANCING

Perhaps the LORD will act on our behalf.
(1 Samuel 14:6)

'Confrontation' is an aspect of life that many of us prefer to avoid. Letting 'sleeping dogs lie', hoping that issues will go away or be resolved by themselves, is our preferred option. But as those whose lives have been touched by God, these are not choices available to us. One of the many promises that Jesus gave to us is that we would have 'trouble' (John 16:33). This means confrontation, both external and within ourselves, against sin, worldliness and the devil.

The Old Testament presents many examples of battles and clashes involving military action and bloody exchanges. But these were not only taking place at an obvious physical level but pointing to a spiritual dimension. Whilst the New Testament features hardly any scenes of combat, the language of vigorous activity and battling still exists. Jesus said, 'the kingdom of heaven has been forcefully advancing and forceful men lay hold of it' (Matthew 11:12). No room for opting out here!

This is where Jonathan, back in the Old Testament, is shown as someone who is ready to act forcefully . . . based on his focusing beyond the horizon. But this is in contrast to his father, King Saul. He is described as 'staying on the outskirts of Gibeah under a pomegranate tree in Migron' (1 Samuel 14:2). On the face of it there were good reasons for Saul's inactivity. The Philistines who confronted him and the Israelites had imposed economic sanctions with the result (as referred to in a previous chapter) that, 'Not a blacksmith could be found in the whole land of Israel.' As a consequence there was a distinct lack of military hardware. Only Saul and Jonathan possessed a sword or spear. The Philistines were also tightening their grip on the nation of Israel, forcing Saul's army to retreat and hold a line further south.

Whilst Jonathan was aware of these factors, he chose to look beyond them. He was focused on God . . . sadly his father was not, rendered immobile by his perception of the situation. But it was Jonathan's focus in the face of this paralysis on the one hand, and overwhelming opposition on the other, that galvanised him for action. He was 'up' for confronting the enemy! *'Jonathan said to his young armour bearer, "Come, let's go over to the outpost of those uncircumcised fellows. Perhaps the LORD will act on our behalf. Nothing can hinder the LORD from saving, whether by many or by few"'* (1 Samuel 14:6). He saw the possibility of God acting and bringing victory despite the hopeless odds. Jonathan then suggested a way of discerning if this was going to be the case at this time. If the enemy soldiers taunted him to come further, then this was to be taken as a sign from God that He would, indeed, act on the Israelites' behalf.

That's what happened. Following the Philistines' response in saying, *'Come up to us and we'll teach you a lesson'*, Jonathan and companion climbed up towards them, not only being empowered to kill twenty soldiers but then seeing a panic sent by God cause their entire army to retreat in disarray. Then Saul, literally and figuratively, woke up to what was happening. His army was able to then take full advantage of the Philistine panic that was leading them to slaughter one another. A great victory ensued (see 1 Samuel 14:20–23).

This all occurred because Jonathan was prepared to confront the enemy and see that things could be different with God's intervention. Whilst we are unlikely to face the same military scenario, we are still in a battle. As the apostle Paul described it, this is a spiritual one against *'the rulers, against the authorities, against the powers of this dark world and against the spiritual forces of evil in the heavenly realms'* (Ephesians 6:12). Rather like Jonathan, we may also feel distinctly vulnerable on account of having limited resources. But, again as Paul states, our weapons are *'not . . . of the world'*. Yet they have *'divine power to demolish strongholds'* (2 Corinthians 10:4).

Prayer is one of these weapons. It is at this point that, like

Jonathan, we are not altogether certain of the outcome; *'perhaps the Lord will act on our behalf'* is how we often feel. But we can be certain of seeing God's specific purposes worked out, whatever the opposition, since *'Nothing can hinder the Lord from saving, whether by many or by few.'* Our part is to 'focus beyond the horizon' as a means of forcefully advancing.

MEN OF ISSACHAR – THE RIGHT TIME

> . . . men of Issachar, who understood the times
> and knew what Israel should do.
> (1 Chronicles 12:32)

Is this the right time? Such a question might arise particularly when faced with life-changing decisions. Moving from education to work, buying a house, leaving a job, getting married, Christian work, retirement . . . All of these and many others involve the element of timing. The consequences can be significant.

Nations and people-groups also come to pivotal points in their history where timing is vital. Israel faced a critical moment following the death of King Saul in battle against the Philistine enemy forces. The way now seemed clear for David to take the crown, having previously been anointed into that role by the prophet Samuel. But he knew that he needed to keep in step with God's timetable. So he asked God, *'Shall I go up to one of the towns of Judah?'* When a positive reply was received, he then asked to which one he was to go. The answer was the town of Hebron (see 2 Samuel 2:1). He was to be content in having to reign over just one tribe of Israel at that time. The remainder of God's people were not yet in a place to receive him.

Then came a time of waiting . . . a long time! For seven years plus! Most of us would have given up or tried to force the pace. But David knew from experience that he needed to wait for God's agenda to be completed. In the meantime he was certain that it was God's ultimate purpose for him to have kingship over the whole nation. Sadly, in our own age where Godly patience and tenacity in holding on are often lacking, we opt for the 'quick fix' and the second best. David's attitude is an encouragement for us to 'keep in there' until complete fulfilment and total blessing is received from God.

But David was not the only one who was waiting. A bloody conflict then took place between those in the nation who wanted the dynasty of King Saul to succeed, and those who recognised David's anointing as king. *'David . . . grew stronger and stronger, while the house of Saul grew weaker and weaker'* (2 Samuel 3:1). As a consequence the other tribes of Israel joined the tribe of Judah in recognising David's rightful status. Amongst those who sent their military forces to come under his command was the tribe of Issachar, who *'understood the times and knew what Israel should do'*.

The men of this tribe had been watching . . . and waiting. In this period of national upheaval, uncertainty, turmoil and contention, they were not considering just the political power struggle that was taking place before their eyes. Their focus was also beyond the horizon. They not only discerned that David was the right man for the role of shepherding God's people at a time when others were manoeuvring for that position, but they also judged when this was to take place. And this was without the aid of Google, Wikipedia or LinkedIn!

The timing was vital, and the prompting as to when to act could only have come from God. To move too soon might have seen the old order still strong enough to prevent a smooth transition. To delay too long and the fledgling monarchy could have been crushed by the alert Philistines on their borders. Nevertheless the latter had a good go at snuffing out David's reign at birth, before being dealt a severe mauling through God's intervention (see 2 Samuel 5:17–25).

The men of Issachar had been looking at a source far better than any website! They were looking to God to show them the right time to step in and lend David their support. As the psalmist was to write: 'The LORD is my light and my salvation' (Psalm 27:1). This is a reminder to us of continuing to focus upon God and similarly await His timing in our lives.

Wait for the Lord; be strong and take heart and wait for the LORD.
(Psalm 27:14)

A WIDOW – NOT TOO OLD

. . . and then was a widow until she was eighty-four.
(Luke 2:37)

'Silver surfers' – those of older years now making use of the internet and associated technology – are an increasingly significant demographic group. Marketing now has to take them into account, and political parties cannot afford to discard them. Employers are also realising the advantages of retaining staff who, in previous years, would have been automatically retired once a landmark age had been reached.

But is the value of those in advancing years to be seen only in their maturity and dependability? These are worthy and positive attributes. But in Luke's Gospel we find descriptions of older people who were to offer even more. The opening chapter gives the account of Zachariah the priest and his barren, now old, wife Elizabeth. However, he failed to focus beyond the horizon of biological restrictions . . . and was duly rebuked by the angel Gabriel who had brought great news of impending parenthood. This was in answer to their prayer. Unfortunately it seemed that either they had forgotten what they had prayed, or felt that their prayer had passed its 'sell-by date'. Hence Zachariah was rendered dumb after voicing his doubts – which was somewhat ironic! Nevertheless they had the joy of bringing John the Baptist into this world who, as a man, prepared the way for Jesus to enter His earthly ministry.

In contrast Luke 2 tells us about a third character in this senior age-group who recognised and responded to what God was doing. It's unfortunate that this account of Anna takes up only three verses and probably grabs our attention only every 12 months at Christmas.

Other people in the temple at the same time as Anna would have simply seen a young, poor couple with their eight-day-old baby going through the Jewish rite of circumcision. But she saw much more . . . and this did not arise by accident. Focusing beyond the horizon and catching hold of what God is doing is not only the outcome of being spiritually sensitive. Although this factor is clearly important, the account of Anna shows something else. The brief details in this narrative point out that, *'She never left the temple but worshipped night and day, fasting and praying'* (Luke 2:37). She was committed to seeking God. Whilst 'commitment' may be a concept that is shunned in our current age, it is still a virtue that needs pursuing. The world of sport contains many examples of men and women totally giving themselves to achieve their ultimate potential. Bobby Moore was the captain of the England World Cup winning soccer team of 1966. He was reckoned to be a good professional footballer but not particularly exceptional.

However, he committed himself to develop into a classy, skilful and perceptive international performer who eventually played over 100 games for his nation. And this was done by training hard, arriving early and being the last to leave every session. Being gifted was not enough.

Anna brings out the spiritual aspect of this lesson. Also, being given the description *'prophetess'*, her devotion enabled her to be in the right place at the right time: *'Coming up to them at that very moment . . .'* As a result she was enabled to recognise that this was no ordinary event but the long-sought provision of God by way of the promised Messiah. He had come not as a warrior-king to bring political freedom for Israel, but as a baby to give His life as the spiritual redeemer for all people. She saw something beyond the purely physical level. Her response to this revelation was to pass on this earth-shattering (and hell-breaking) news to others who would appreciate its significance.

Waiting for this event had been worthwhile – in Anna's case it had been the length of her widowhood, possibly 84 years. But she had consistently kept her focus, and age had not been a barrier to being able to see beyond the horizon. There was no 'retirement' for her . . . or us. Indeed when such an age is eventually reached it seems, as with Zechariah, Elizabeth and Anna, that this is the point where things start getting really interesting!

BARNABAS – GOING AGAINST THE FLOW

He was a good man, full of the Holy Spirit and faith . . .
(Acts 11:24)

The man that he saw was viewed as a fanatic, murderer and virulent enemy, the equivalent of our modern-day Islamic State terrorist. But Barnabas saw something different. At a pivotal point in the life of the early Church there had arisen a violent and fearful persecution of believers. This had been initiated following the stoning to death of Stephen – a bold and unflinching witness to Jesus being the true Messiah. It had been instigated by that man named Saul. The account puts it starkly: *'On that day a great persecution broke out against the church at Jerusalem, and all except the apostles were scattered throughout Judea and Samaria . . . But Saul began to destroy the church. Going from house to house, he dragged off men and women and put them into prison'* (Acts 8:1, 3). Saul did not stop there, as he is then described as *'breathing out murderous threats'* and asking for permission to broaden his mission to include Damascus, *'so that if he found any there who belonged to the Way, whether men or women, he might take them as prisoners to Jerusalem'* (9:1–2).

The conversion of Saul, also called Paul (Acts 13:9), on that road to Damascus marked an amazing change in the work and witness of God's church. It also presented a problem. Ananias, the disciple to whom Jesus appeared with a command to go to Paul within days of the latter's conversion, voiced the concern that had now arisen: *'I have heard many reports about this man and all the harm he has done to your saints in Jerusalem. And he has come here with authority from the chief priests to arrest all who call on your name'* (Acts 9:13–14). Others shared this feeling and confusion, such that when Paul arrived back in Jerusalem (having had to escape from Damascus by means of a basket put over the town wall because of death threats), we are told: *'they were all afraid of him, not believing that he really was a disciple'* (Acts 9:26). This was where Barnabas comes centre stage. It is also where he goes against the flow. Instead of being fearful and suspicious, he got alongside Paul, recognising that he was God's *'chosen instrument'* (see Acts 9:15).

Barnabas was focusing beyond the horizon in not judging Paul in the same way as others. He had something of a 'track record' in stepping out into uncharted territory. Earlier he had voluntarily sold a field that he had owned and placed the money he received into the apostles' hands (see Acts 4:36–37). Now, in this new situation, he again took a bold step. He took Paul to the apostles and related his conversion encounter with the risen Jesus and subsequent fearless preaching. This validation was clearly enough for the church leaders who embraced Paul as a true brother and integrated him into the life of the Church.

But Barnabas did not stop there. Perhaps the other leaders had not seen Paul's full potential . . . or perhaps they were still cautious. So when Barnabas was sent to check the evangelism now taking place amongst the non-Jews some years later, he returned from Antioch with a very positive report . . . then went straight off to get Paul back from Tarsus (see Acts 11:20–25). It was when they were together again in Antioch amongst the other prophets and teachers that God moved things up a gear. The Holy Spirit spoke in a specific way, directing that Paul was to be set aside for special work . . . and that this was to be done alongside Barnabas (see Acts 13:1–3). This was the start of what subsequently became labelled as 'Paul's first missionary journey'. Other journeys followed, with letters subsequently being written to churches and individual leaders whom Paul needed to mentor. These writings continue to be used by God to impact us today. But none of this would have been possible if Barnabas had not gone against the flow of what others were thinking, and seen Paul in a very different light as he focused beyond the horizon.

It was prophesied of Jesus that, *'He will not judge by what he sees with his eyes, or decide by what he hears with his ears; but with righteousness he will judge the needy, with justice he will give decisions for the poor of the earth'* (Isaiah 11:3−4). It was with that same Spirit that Barnabas 'saw' something in Paul that others had not seen. On that point it is perhaps a good way to end this study. We can so easily be critical and come to wrong conclusions about other people. But Barnabas didn't; certainly Jesus didn't. Just as we saw that Samuel needed to focus beyond the horizon in terms of David actually being the next king of Israel, and Barnabas was able to see Paul as the apostle, so Jesus looks at you and me in a different way from how others view us . . . or even as we view ourselves. He sees us as those whom He consistently and faithfully loves . . . and for whom He has purposes yet to be fulfilled. So let's keep focusing!

> 'No eye has seen, no ear has heard, no mind has conceived what
> God has prepared for those who love him' − but God has
> revealed it to us by his Spirit.
> (1 Corinthians 2:9−10)

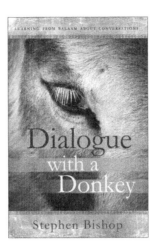

DIALOGUE WITH A DONKEY
Learning from Balaam about conversations
Stephen Bishop

A talking donkey and sword-wielding angel are the images most commonly associated with the Old Testament character of Balaam. Yet the significance and relevance of this account seem to be rarely considered.

"Dialogue with a Donkey" aims to open up this extraordinary story by looking at other conversations that were taking place… and which continue to do so. The compelling force of words to specifically direct, challenge, influence, affirm and develop people's lives are considered through Balaam's successive utterances. These pronouncements brought a divine perspective to the Israelites at that time. As this book advocates, we also need to hear what God is saying, breaking through all surrounding voices. It also underlines how Balaam's words reached a climax in pointing to Jesus who continues powerfully speaking into our darkness.

The stubborn donkey ends up being the means by which other people had God's life-giving word brought to them. We also need to hear such words. Are we listening?

£4.99 GBP / $7.99 USD / $8.99 AUD
ISBN 9781909824256
5.5 x 8.5" Paperback
Published by Zaccmedia

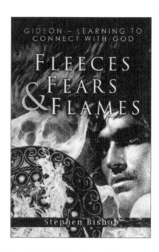

FLEECES, FEARS AND FLAMES

Gideon – Learning to connect with God

Stephen Bishop

Gideon is a well-known Bible character. His exploits in leading just three hundred men to defeat a huge invading army has inspired many people when faced with situations which are 'against-all-odds'. But how did it occur? Where was God in this scenario? How does this account relate to us?

'Fleeces, fears and flames' explores the Book of Judges in order to examine these ques-tions. Written in a down-to-earth manner, it looks at God connecting with Gideon despite his fears and fleece-laying doubts, then breaking through such frailty to release his power as seen in those flames. But it also shows that God is able to connect and work in our lives however daunting the challenges confronting us!

Suitable for individual reflection or group discussion, this material includes questions and a focus at the end of each main chapter to help connect the Biblical narrative in a personal way.

£4.99 GBP / $7.99 USD / $8.99 AUD
ISBN 9781909824492
5.5 x 8.5" Paperback
Published by Zaccmedia

Lightning Source UK Ltd.
Milton Keynes UK
UKOW06f1402100815

256690UK00001B/10/P

9 781909 824737